FORAGING WILD EDIBLE PLANTS
OF NORTH AMERICA

FORAGING WILD EDIBLE PLANTS OF NORTH AMERICA

More Than 150 Delicious Recipes Using Nature's Edibles

Second Edition

Christopher Nyerges

ESSEX, CONNECTICUT

FALCONGUIDES®

An imprint of Globe Pequot, the trade division of
The Rowman & Littlefield Publishing Group, Inc.
4501 Forbes Blvd., Ste. 200
Lanham, MD 20706
www.rowman.com

Falcon and FalconGuides are registered trademarks and Make Adventure Your Story is a trademark of The Rowman & Littlefield Publishing Group, Inc.

Distributed by NATIONAL BOOK NETWORK

British Library Cataloguing-in-Publication Information available

Library of Congress Cataloging-in-Publication Data

Names: Nyerges, Christopher, author.
Title: Foraging wild edible plants of North America : more than 150 delicious recipes using nature's edibles / Christopher Nyerges.
Other titles: Falcon guide.
Description: Second edition. | Essex, Connecticut : FalconGuides, [2023] | Series: A Falcon guide | Includes bibliographical references and index. | Summary: "A full-color field and feast guide with images of the most common edible wild plants, complete with recipes and folklore"— Provided by publisher.
Identifiers: LCCN 2022039801 (print) | LCCN 2022039802 (ebook) | ISBN 9781493064472 (paperback) | ISBN 9781493064489 (epub)
Subjects: LCSH: Wild plants, Edible—North America. | Wild foods—North America. | Cooking (Wild foods). | Field guides. | Illustrated works. | Cookbooks.
Classification: LCC TX369 .N94 2023 (print) | LCC TX369 (ebook) | DDC 641.3/02—dc23/eng/20220831
LC record available at https://lccn.loc.gov/2022039801
LC ebook record available at https://lccn.loc.gov/2022039802

∞™ The paper used in this publication meets the minimum requirements of American National Standard for Information Sciences—Permanence of Paper for Printed Library Materials, ANSI/NISO Z39.48-1992.

To all those who provide sustenance
instead of merely making meals
this book is dedicated.

CONTENTS

WHY THIS BOOK?

Most of the plants included in this book are widely distributed and can be found in most parts of North America, especially the United States. There are a few exceptions to this, and we'll tell you about them when you read the properties of each plant. A few are natives of the West or the East, but most are imports from Europe and elsewhere. The common weeds are the ubiquitous inhabitants of vacant lots, plowed fields, edges of farmland, and backyards.

Greens are not sufficient to keep you alive by themselves, but they provide the vitamins and minerals that your body needs. Greens liven up soups, salads, and MRE dishes, and anything made from dehydrated or stored foods. Greens are the staff of life, and they can be included in any recipe that calls for spinach, watercress, or lettuce. Yes, some have distinct flavors and textures, and yes, some may require some getting used to.

For this new edition we've also included those fruits, nuts, and seeds that are the most widespread in North America.

The plants that we profile here, and the recipes we provide, are an easy way to get started with regularly using wild foods and introducing them into your family's diet.

AN INTRODUCTION TO WILD PLANTS

Before agriculture and the tilling of the soil, we hunted and foraged for wild plants. Collecting wild plants for our meals was second nature; it was just as "normal" as modern people opening the refrigerator door.

As specific plants became locally favored, we began to centralize, manipulate, and domesticate these wild plants near our living areas. It has been speculated that agriculture began unintentionally when early man observed that certain plants grew in and around the community's manure piles. The hardy survivor plants were those whose seeds passed through the human body and still sprouted and grew.

In any event, it was certainly more convenient to have these hardier food plants growing near the community where they could be easily harvested. The gradual selection and domestication of a certain few groups of plants eventually allowed civilizations to flourish and flower.

And while mankind was able to devote more time to crafts and arts, the "wild ones" were increasingly ignored.

But they were not forgotten! The knowledge, use, and lore of wild plants have been kept alive not just by Indian historians and botanists but by all the peoples everywhere who have suffered hard times. During such hard times, those who have retained the knowledge of the old ways know that whenever their society failed them, they could turn to the earth to provide simple, and usually adequate, sustenance.

North American Indians collected and used wild plants as a regular, day-to-day activity. It was a part of life. Until relatively recent centuries, the Indians fully utilized the gifts of nature. They freely shared their hard-earned knowledge with the European colonists, and many colonists owed their very survival to these indigenous people. (And how was the favor repaid?)

The manner in which the indigenous California people practiced "agriculture" with wild plants has been well documented in the book *Tending the Wild* by M. Kat Anderson. Many of these techniques were practiced widely, not just in California, such as the use of fire, digging sticks, and pruning, so that wild plants produced reliably. It was an intensive, complex combination of ways of dealing with the land on a large scale that was the rival of modern agriculture.

Wild foods have been used during wartime when normal food production is curtailed or focused on military needs. During a war or an economic depression, when diet may be dictated by food lines and ration coupons, wild foods are a welcome supplement.

I've spoken with many people whose survival during World War II was partially dependent on their ability to gather local wild foods. As one German woman told me, "Yes, we were as thin as sticks. There was no food! But the cattail, nettles, and other wild plants kept us alive. That's all there was!"

When food is abundant, we tend to forget the harsh realities that visit us periodically and predictably. In our myopia during these times of plenty, we pave over the food-producing areas, cut down the food-producing trees in favor of pointless ornamentals, and vigorously poison our lawns and gardens to kill off the last dandelion and chickweed in the name of order and beauty. How sad that so many of us have chosen to ignore our roots!

Hoboes have romanticized the lifestyle of the traveling man, free from the restrictions of the dominant society. The hobo, although usually seen as a bum, loafer, freeloader, alcoholic, and generally a burden on society, was also romantically seen as a member of the loose brotherhood of wandering nomads. The life of the hobo, whether chosen or a matter of circumstance, was hard but generally self-reliant. The hobo found his food in an orchard, in a breadline, in a trashcan, as barter for work, and of course, from all the freely growing weeds, shrubs, and trees from coast to coast, from border to border and beyond. To survive, the hobo utilized *all* the "free" resources available to him. (And yes, I am well aware that such vagabonds are not generally liked by most members of society.)

And don't forget the contribution that unemployment and poverty have made to keeping the knowledge of wild food plants alive. When that check stops coming in, wild foods can be used to fill the gap.

One morning I sat with a friend on the front steps of his home. He had been laid off from his job a few weeks earlier and, barely able to pay the rent, he just didn't have any money to buy food. He was hungry, he told me, and hadn't eaten much in three days. I asked him if he was using the food from his yard. His response was great laughter, not as ridicule, but as he put it, because he needed "real food."

"Let's look around," I suggested. We walked around his yard gathering edible plants. It was spring and the yard was abundant with young weeds, since he never bothered to mow the lawn and pull weeds. We collected enough wild foods to make a large salad and several cooked vegetables. We even picked fresh guava fruits from the backyard ornamental tree that my friend didn't know was there. The salad was simple but alive. The greens and vegetables, steamed and buttered, were vibrant and delicious. The fruits were sweet, like manna from heaven.

My friend was surprised that all this was in his small urban backyard. Now he saw that the weeds in his yard were valuable resources. They were not just bothersome growths that had to be pulled up and thrown away. Instead of token substitutes for "real food," my friend saw that these plants of the earth were, indeed, real food.

Campers and hunters have also traditionally kept alive the lore of plant foods. These plants helped to keep the pack light when hiking. They could also be relied upon if one became lost or stranded.

But let's not see these wild plants as only "food as a last resort" when you're in a survival situation. That is too limited a viewpoint. Wild plants are a resource that we should get to know and appreciate on a day-to-day basis. Include them in your meals today. Why wait for tomorrow?

Wild foods, for most of us during "normal" times, will usually not play the dominant or primary role in our diet. But do consider some of the advantages of including them in your daily meals, along with fresh garden produce and store-bought foods. No fresher salad can be made than one that is gathered minutes before dinner. Fresh, green, leafy, wild salad plants are the most nutritious and healthful, not having been subjected to commercial fertilizers, pesticides, or long storage periods.

Wild foods are often useful substitutes or extenders of other food items. However, most of their flavors, textures, and aromas are unique; therefore these plants should be considered valid foods themselves, not only as "substitutes."

Another important reason to use wild plants is that this practice keeps us constantly aware of the fact that the earth does provide for all its inhabitants. Our modern, man-made system of food production and distribution "works" but is ever subject to manipulation and disruption by a variety of political and economic factors. Furthermore, as more and more of us depend on big agriculture for our food, fewer and fewer farmers are doing the actual work, and the land is plowed and denuded and sprayed with pesticides in the name of "food production." If you want greater clarity in wrapping your mind around what we do to the land in the name of agriculture, take the time to read *The One-Straw Revolution* by Masanobu Fukuoka. It's a real eye-opener.

Using wild food plants not only has immediate value but also keeps us prepared for possible crises that may affect our food supply.

Edible, Medicinal, and Poisonous Plants

Reprinted with permission of Tom Elpel

Often wild foods affect our body differently from either garden or store-bought foods. Using wild foods on a regular basis, combined with our other food items, keeps the body attuned to these more basic foods. Should we suddenly be forced to subsist largely on wild plants, our bodies will be somewhat adjusted. Also remember, many people have remained hungry, malnourished, and have even died when wild foods were abundant. They simply could not "stomach" such foods—at least they believed they couldn't. A prejudiced viewpoint can ultimately be our greatest enemy.

Wild Food Outings and Workshops

I have taught thousands of city dwellers that wild foods abound not only in faraway green pastures but right in alleys, vacant lots, and backyards. Since I started teaching in 1974 under the encouragement of the nonprofit WTI, I've taken many groups of people on weekend outings to identify the locally growing plants. We've always been able to make at least a salad and tea from whatever we've found on our short excursions. Sampling a few wild plants in delicious recipes, right then and there, has been a valuable experience for all the attendees of the outings. For many, the knowledge of wild foods had been strictly intellectual up to that point. Now they were actually tasting and drinking, discovering new flavors and monitoring different body reactions. Not only has this had a dramatic personal impact on all the outing participants, but it has also added a more realistic dimension to any discussion of "how the Indians lived."

During special wild food workshops, we've made full meals, letting the participants do most of the work so they can get a feel for actually working with these plants. These workshops are conducted at a park, a public building, or at someone's home. We begin by going on a short walk, and then collecting many of the ingredients for our meal that day, with the participants doing the actual gathering. We don't "plan" a particular menu but let whatever is in season do the planning. That way, the entire experience for the participants is much more real, not artificial.

Once we've collected everything that we'll be using, we lay out the plants on tables. Participants will begin cleaning and preparing the plants, under supervision. Others will work on getting a fire started and developing a good bed of coals.

Often prickly pear cactus pads will be peeled and diced and someone will begin sautéing them. This will become a delicious prickly pear omelet once the cactus is cooked and onions and eggs are added. It is served with a dash of hot sauce. A cactus, onion, and tomato stew can also be cooked.

Watercress soup will be made by finely chopping the greens and letting them simmer in a pot of milk. Seasoned with paprika, this is a grand soup for any occasion.

At these wild food workshops, we always make a salad and several steamed greens. We'll make tea from sage, bay, Mormon tea, mint, or whatever else may be available.

Our usual bread is acorn bread. Acorns require a thorough leaching before using the flour for bread, so I've usually brought shelled, leached, and dried acorns to the workshops to save time. In some cases when we've allocated more time, I've brought raw acorns and let the participants peel them and begin boiling and leaching them, so the students see the entire process from beginning to end. (Note: The complete leaching process for acorns is discussed in detail in my *Foraging California* and *Guide to Wild Foods and Useful Plants* books.)

The leached acorns are ground to a flour and then used in bread or pancake batter. The bread can be baked in a solar oven or in a covered pan over the coals of a fire. The pancakes are cooked on a buttered cast-iron skillet.

Boiled cattail spikes (eaten like corn on the cob) are a tasty addition to our workshop meals when in season, as are all the other edible parts of the cattail.

For dessert, we have teas and various wild fruits such as prickly pear cactus, carob pods, currants, and whatever other fruits are in season. Occasionally we'll make prickly pear cactus fruit ice cream, carob brownies, currant jam, and so on.

We don't usually prepare any meat items during our workshops. Our protein is usually derived from milk, cheese, and eggs added to the wild ingredients. Sometimes, however, we've tested such delicacies as snails (escargot), worms, grasshoppers, termite larvae, rattlesnakes, and other "meat" sources.

ABOUT THE RECIPES

Many of the recipes in this book can be adapted and changed to fit whatever is in season or available wherever you happen to be. Don't feel restricted. Experiment. Try new variations and combinations.

The recipes in this book are generally very simple. In most of the recipes, wild foods are the dominant ingredients. This is so you can experience and get to know each particular plant. It isn't to suggest that there is anything wrong with not using wild foods as the main ingredients—but you should know each plant well before you can determine how to best use it and how not to use it.

Never forget that regardless of how complicated a recipe you might develop, all of these wild food plants can usually be enjoyed simply raw or steamed if circumstances dictate simplicity. In fact, most wild foods are at their best unadorned and uncluttered. See these wild plants as the wonderful foods they are—simple, direct, primal.

You may come to realize that modern man is missing this gift of the earth by our almost exclusive preference for the pampered foods of hybridization. As you slowly chew, let these plants that have nurtured bygone civilizations nurture you. Let the full implications of the bounty all around become readily apparent to you, and welcome these "weeds" as your allies and friends.

WHAT TO CARRY WHEN HIKING

The addition of a few items and ingredients to your daypack will enable you to make delicious dishes at day's end.

Utensils

I've often carried along a small salad bowl to make salad production more convenient. However, if you need to save weight and space, just use a sturdy plastic bag. It folds down small and weighs little. When you're ready to make a salad, simply open the bag, fold the edges over, and add the various ingredients. Tossing the salad is easy—just close the bag and shake. And I must admit, I often carry a jar of salad dressing, usually just an oil and vinegar mix.

For a cooking pot, I use a small stainless steel pot, a small cast-iron skillet or pot, or an enamelware pot. Aluminum is lightweight and inexpensive and ubiquitous at the camping supply stores. However, aluminum is toxic to the body and it readily leaches both acids and alkalies. The aluminum industry still states that aluminum poisoning is an old wives' tale, but there has been far too much data collected over the past hundred years to prove the contrary. (Yes, I'm aware that there's still debate and controversy over this one, but I've discussed the physiological effects of aluminum elsewhere, in my *Urban Wilderness* book, Peace Press, 1979. Still, I suggest that you avoid the use of aluminum in cooking utensils wherever possible.)

Incidentally, you can cook and boil water in a paper cup or a small birch bark cooking pot. Why doesn't the paper burn? The water in the cup keeps the temperature of the paper below the burning point. In a pinch this is a good fact to know. And on some of our outings, we've hollowed out the dried flowering stalk of the yucca plant, and after setting it on the ground horizontally, we'd fill it with water. We'd heat that water (or soup) by adding very hot rocks to the liquid using tongs.

Also don't forget hobo ingenuity. An old can, cleaned out and hung over a fire or straddled over two stones in the hot coals, serves as a fine cooking pot.

For eating utensils, carry small bowls, metal sierra cups, or, if need be, use a flat rock for a "dish." I carry small wooden bowls, which are lightweight and a pleasure to use.

I'd much rather eat with heavier and more rugged silverware than lightweight plastic utensils that break when you bend them wrong. If you insist on the lightweight plastic utensils, I'd suggest unbreakable Lexan forks and spoons.

But one needn't panic if there is no fork or spoon in your pack. Use chopsticks! I often carry a pair, and they are easy for eating everything except soup. If you don't carry a pair along, make a pair. Cut two segments from a mature cattail stalk or two equal-length segments from any straight piece of nonpoisonous wood, such as mulefat. Soon you will discover that the woods are full of chopsticks.

Condiments

For seasoning the wild food dishes that you collect along the trail, there are a few simple, lightweight items that really make the meal more enjoyable. I often carry oil and vinegar in my pack in separate containers. This way I can use just the oil for frying or sautéing, and I can still combine the oil and vinegar when needed for salad dressing.

The oil and vinegar can be carried in any waterproof container. I've used plastic 35mm film containers (though you hardly see them anymore) and old vitamin pill containers, and these work quite well. Small glass or plastic spice and pill bottles are also useful containers, but be careful with glass.

Salt Substitutes

Salt makes a great difference in the flavor, palatability, and enjoyment of many food dishes. Salt has been so valued over the millennia that it was often traded over long distances. In the Roman Empire, salt was actually used as money. ("Salt" is the root of the word "salary.") If you don't have salt, or if you choose not to use it for health reasons, there are substitutes. The best salt substitute is seaweed. Seaweeds provide potassium chloride, instead of the sodium chloride that table salt provides. Virtually any fresh, nonrotting seaweed can be collected, dried, powdered, and used as you'd use salt. The flavor is similar, but milder, than regular salt.

No seaweed available? The leaves of all species of *Atriplex*, commonly called saltbush, can be dried, powdered, and used like salt. However, you need to experiment because some species are better than others. Sometimes the dried leaves of saltbush are burned and the ashes used like salt. Try this and decide for yourself.

The related *Chenopodium* genus (whose most notable member is lamb's-quarters) can also be used this way. But once again, you will need to experiment. Even some of the *Chenopodiums* can be strong-flavored.

For seasoning, some herbs can be dried and powdered, and used in combinations to flavor salads and cooked greens. The more pungent and flavorful herbs are best for this purpose. These include watercress (and all members of the Mustard family), various sages, rosemary, onions, the small red fruits of the California pepper tree (ground), and licorice-flavored fennel seeds.

Sprouts

Sprouts are a nutritious addition to salad and cooked foods. Occasionally sprouts can be collected fresh from the wild by looking under older plants whose seeds have dropped. Try this in the spring when new plants are coming up and year-round along warm coastlines.

Wild seeds can be collected and sprouted, as can any seeds you may have in your pack (or stored in your cupboard). The usual way to sprout seeds at home is simple. Soak the seeds overnight. In the morning, drain the water and keep the seeds in a jar with a screen or cloth lid. Keep the jar on its side in a dark place, and flush the seeds with water about three or four times a day. The seeds will begin to sprout and grow, and they'll be ready to be eaten in about 5 to 10 days, depending on the variety of seed.

You needn't buy a special sprouting jar in order to make sprouts. Just get an old mayonnaise or pickle jar. For a lid, use a piece of clean cotton cloth secured with a rubber band.

Making sprouts on the trail can be as simple as at home if you carry a plastic sprouting jar. If this seems too cumbersome to you, try using plastic bags. The seeds to be sprouted are placed in a cloth, which is placed in a plastic bag. This plastic bag is then placed in another plastic bag for safe carrying. As before, begin by soaking the seeds overnight. Then rinse with water three or four times daily, until the sprouts are large enough to eat. If readers know of other good ways to make sprouts in the backcountry, please write and let me know.

Sprouts are an excellent addition to salads, sandwiches, soups, and various cooked dishes.

WHY WILD FOODS?

There is no doubt that "hard times"—whether due to war, pandemics, natural calamities, economic hardships, or being lost in the wilderness—are difficult, stressful, and taxing on our physical and mental well-being. Knowledge of wild foods is only one of a vast number of tools that help to make one a survivor and not a listing in an obituary column. The use of wild plants should by no means be limited to your wilderness travels. Survival situations can and do occur anywhere under a broad variety of circumstances, even in all major cities of the world.

It is wise to personally develop all the various survival skills and to practice these wherever possible in our daily lives. This is not simply to be ready for emergencies. We eat wild foods to genuinely improve the quality of our lives, and our health.

Berries

STRAWBERRIES (*Fragaria* spp.)

Strawberries are part of the Rose family (Rosaceae). *Fragaria* contains 20 species worldwide. The following three are most common throughout the United States:

BEACH STRAWBERRY (*Fragaria chiloensis*)

Found along beaches and coastal grasslands. Receptacle about 10 to 20 mm. Leaf petiole generally 2 to 20 cm.

WOOD STRAWBERRY (*Fragaria vesca*)

Found in partial shade in the forests. Receptacle about 5 to 10 mm. Leaf petiole generally 3 to 25 cm.

MOUNTAIN STRAWBERRY (*Fragaria virginiana*)

Found in the higher elevations in meadows and forest clearings. Receptacle more or less about 10 mm. Leaf petiole generally 1 to 25 cm.

IDENTIFYING STRAWBERRIES

If you've grown strawberries in your yard, you will be able to recognize wild strawberries. Though there are 20 species worldwide, you're going to find maybe three different species in North America whose leaves and fruits are very similar, the difference typically being the size.

Fruit of the wild strawberry (*Fragaria vesca*). PHOTO BY DR. AMADEJ TRNKOCZY.

Strawberry leaves are all basal, generally three-lobed leaves, each leaflet having fine teeth.

The fruit of the strawberry is what botanists call an aggregate accessory fruit, meaning that the fleshy part is derived not from the plant's ovaries but from the receptacle that holds the ovaries. In other words, what we call "the fruit" (because, duh!, it looks like a fruit) is the receptacle, and all the little seeds on the outside of the "fruit" are technically referred to as achenes, actually one of the ovaries of the flower, with a seed inside it. It sounds complicated, but again, if you've ever seen a cultivated strawberry, you know what a strawberry looks like!

When the average person sees one, especially if it's summer and the plant is in fruit, they will typically say, "Hey, look, isn't that a wild strawberry?"

USES

Strawberries are so widely known that just about everyone recognizes them when they see them, even though the wild varieties are significantly smaller than the

Wild strawberry flowers and leaves. PHOTO BY JEAN PAWEK.

huge ones that can be found in the markets. Wild strawberries are between ¼ and ½ inch long. A ½ inch wild strawberry is a big one! Though they may be smaller, the wild ones are typically sweeter, firmer, and tastier.

All indigenous peoples used wild strawberries, eating them fresh, sometimes cooking them, sometimes drying them for later.

You use these in every way that you'd use cultivated strawberries. Eat them as is, dry them, make into jams and jellies, put on top of ice cream and pancakes, etc.

Strawberry leaf tea (made by infusion), though not strongly flavored, is popular in many circles. It is high in vitamin C, and is a mild diuretic with astringent properties.

Moundsville Bush Beverage

Handful of ripe wild strawberries
1 cup cold spring water
1 teaspoon honey

Crush or chop the berries and add them to the water and stir. Stir in the honey.

Ground cover of wild strawberry.

Strawberry Pie Filling

1 cup fresh strawberries, crushed
Sugar to taste
2 tablespoons cornstarch (you can experiment with substituting tapioca, agar, or other thickening agent)
1 cup water

Note: Back before we knew how bad white sugar is for our bodies, everyone recommended it. Yes, it "tastes good," and yes, it is a preservative. However, I suggest you go slow on the sugar, and try other "natural" sugars such as dark honey or date sugar.

Place the strawberries and "sugar" into your saucepan, at low heat. Add the water and cornstarch and cook until you get your desired consistency. You can also add bits of sliced strawberries to the filling.

Lakeside Pondering (Strawberry Leaf Tea)

Collect strawberry leaves, dry them in the shade, and store appropriately for future use. Fresh leaves can also be used.

Add the leaves to your pot or cup, and pour near-boiling water over the leaves. Cover the cup or pot.

Drink when cool. This is often used just for the subtle flavor, as well as an old-fashioned cold remedy. If the flavor is too subtle for you, add mint leaves to the leaves.

WILD CHERRIES (*Prunus* spp.)

Wild cherries are members of the Rose family, which contains 110 genera and 3,000 species worldwide.

Wild cherries are members of the *Prunus* genus, of which there are about 400 species worldwide. Some names of the *Prunus* genus include cherry, almond, apricot, and plum. Here, we're only concerned with those species of *Prunus* that are called cherries.

IDENTIFYING WILD CHERRIES

Wild cherries are very common throughout North America. Though the trees can sometimes grow large, they are typically bushes or tall bushes. They can be evergreen or deciduous (dropping their leaves in winter).

These produce their fruit most abundantly in August. They can be found throughout wild areas, and nearly as commonly in urban areas.

The fruits are typically shiny, dark green, with few to many pointed edges on the leaves, depending on variety.

The tree develops clusters of creamy-white flowers in the spring, and the green fruits begin to develop in early summer. By about August (depending on the location, weather, amount of rain, etc.), the fruits mature to a color that ranges from a pink tone to a deep dark red to nearly black in some cases.

Fruit of the Catalina Island wild cherry, common in western states.

The leaf of the Catalina Island cherry, which is an evergreen.

Leaf of *Prunus virginiana*. PHOTO BY LOUIS-M. LANDRY.

Fruit of the common wild cherry, *Prunus virginiana*, common throughout North America.
PHOTO BY LOUIS-M. LANDRY.

A bowl of the shelled seeds of wild cherry.

One way to identify the plant is to crush the leaves, wait a few seconds, and then smell them. They will have a distinct aroma of bitter almond extract, your clue that the leaf contains "cyanide" (hydrocyanic acid).

Most of the fruits are very much like cultivated cherries, though most are smaller. Also, their color is typically darker red, almost maroon, sometimes even

Fruit and leaf of the Catalina Island cherry, common in the West.

darker. The flesh layer can be very thin in dry years, and thicker in the seasons following a good rain.

Like domestic cherries, there is a thin shell and the meaty inside of the seed.

USES

You can pick the fruits and eat the flesh for a trail snack. If ripe, they're sweet and succulent if it was a wet season. In dry seasons, the flesh is thin, somewhat dry, and a bit tart.

The fruits can be cooked and the seeds removed. The pulp of the fruit can be made into jams or preserves, and even used as a tasty and traditional cough syrup. My favorite from this wild fruit is fruit leather, made by spreading the slightly cooked fruit pulp onto cookie sheets and laying it in the sun until dry.

Native Americans ate the fruit fresh, and sometimes mixed it with meat. Also, the seed ("pit") was considered an important food source. The seeds would be shelled and the meat removed. The inside is then boiled, and the water changed. One boiling is probably sufficient, but I always change the water at least twice just to be safe. Then you can taste the seeds. They have a sweet, nutty flavor. You can mash or grind these seeds and add to soup for a sweet gravy. Or you can dry and grind into a flour, and then mix the flour about 50/50 with other flour for breads, biscuits, or pancakes.

Other members of the *Prunus* genus were used in a similar fashion to the above description, such as *Prunus subcordata*, also known as the Sierra plum, whose yellow to dark red fruit was eaten fresh or dried by various tribes, mostly in northern California. Some tribes removed the pulp of this fruit and dried the pulp into little cakes.

Rick's Repast

A large bowl of ripe, and washed, wild cherries

This is a simple, seat-of-the-pants recipe. Wash the cherries, set them out, and people will eat them. (Save the seeds if you want to try one of the other recipes.)

Cherry Chiller

5 cups ripe cherries
Water, as needed
Honey, to taste

Remove the stems of 5 cups of cherries, and rinse them of any dirt and debris. Put them into a pot and cover with spring water.

Bring them to a soft boil, then gently mash the fruits, using a tool such as a potato masher.

Turn off the heat, cover, and let the fruits simmer for about a half-hour. Then strain the liquid through a colander or cheesecloth. The liquid at this stage might have a hint of bitterness, and if you don't care for that, add a small amount of honey, to taste.

Serve cold.

SERVES APPROXIMATELY FOUR.

Looking Back, Facing Forward (a Pancake from Cherry Seeds)

1 cup of shelled cherry seeds
1 cup of whole-grain pancake mix
Water (or almond milk), as needed
Olive oil

Put the shelled cherry seeds in a pot and cover with water.

Gently boil for about 15 minutes. When the mixture has the general consistency of refried beans, add a cup of your chosen pancake mix.

Next, stir in water or almond milk until you get the appropriate thickness for making pancakes.

Oil your skillet with olive oil, and make your pancakes.

SERVES APPROXIMATELY FOUR.

BLACKBERRIES/RASPBERRIES (*Rubus* spp.)

Blackberries and raspberries are members of the Rose family (Rosaceae). The Rose family contains 110 genera and 3,000 species worldwide.

Blackberries and raspberries belong to the *Rubus* genus, and there are about 400 to 750 species of *Rubus* worldwide.

California blackberry (*Rubus ursinus*) is common in the West. The thimbleberry (*Rubus parviflorus*) and the salmonberry (*Rubus spectabilis*) are widespread. The Himalayan blackberry (*Rubus armeniacus*) is common, widespread, and often regarded as an invasive pest.

IDENTIFYING BLACKBERRIES AND OTHER *RUBUS* SPECIES

Everyone recognizes blackberries, don't they? Blackberries are found all over the world and are widely recognized for their edible berries.

The leaves are palmately divided (like a hand) into three, five, or seven segments. The vines are twining on the ground, or over low hedges, and are characterized by their thorns, which makes it difficult to wade too deep into any of the old hedge-like stands of wild blackberries.

Sometimes people confuse poison oak with blackberry vines, but poison oak lacks the spines. In the spring, the blackberry vines are full of five-petaled white flowers, the ovary of which develops into the characteristic aggregate fruit by early to mid-summer.

The fruits are aggregate fruits, which seem to be universally recognized. The aggregate fruit is a collection of sweet drupelets, with the fruit separating from the flower stalk to form a somewhat hollow, thimble-like shape.

Very few people hesitate when they see a ripe blackberry.

A view of the Himalayan blackberry flowers. PHOTO BY LILY JANE TSONG.

The immature fruit of Himalayan blackberry. PHOTO BY LILY JANE TSONG.

One ripe blackberry fruit. The ripe fruits turn nearly black, and are picked off easily.
PHOTO BY LILY JANE TSONG.

USES

Fruits of all these can be used fresh, sun-dried, in jams and jellies, in puddings, mixed with other nuts and berries for various dishes, as a sweetener, as a juice, in pies, etc.

Nearly every cookbook has several recipes for making blackberry jam or pies. These days, most people enjoy them fresh on cereal or yogurt, or added to a pancake batter. They're also pretty good added to ice cream.

Whether you pick them wild, buy them at the market, or grow them in your own backyard, you can use them all in whatever manner suits you. If you have more than you can eat right away, you can freeze them, or keep them in the refrigerator. You can also try drying some for when the fresh ones are out of season.

Native peoples ate these fruits fresh, and sometimes dried them for winter use. Some indigenous peoples in the old days would collect the half-ripe berries and soak them in water to make what would have been a lemonade-type drink.

Barbara's Blackberry Jam

8 cups blackberries
1 cup apple juice
1 package pectin
3 cups sugar

Mix together the 8 cups of blackberries with the cup of apple juice, and blend in the pectin.

Bring to a boil, stirring continuously.

Add the 3 cups of sugar and stir for another minute or so. Then pour into clean jars, following the usual protocol for home canning.

Note: If you choose to use a more healthful sugar than white sugar, such as maguey syrup or date sugar, experiment first and observe how the mixture thickens. Barbara Kolander has tried many sugar alternatives in her wild food cooking classes, with varied results.

Also note: This is a very basic method for making jam from any fruit, wild or domestic.

LEAF INFUSION

According to Gregory Tilford, author of *Edible and Medicinal Plants of the West*, both the leaves and flowers of these species can be used as an infusion both because of their flavor, and their vitamin and mineral content. Tilford cautions that one should only use the fresh or completely dry leaves for this infusion.

Made into an infusion, the leaf tea can be used to treat cases of mild diarrhea. Gargling with an infusion of blackberry leaf is also good for mouth irritations, such as bleeding gums or sore throat.

Greens

AMARANTH (*Amaranthus* spp.)

Amaranth is a member of the Amaranth family (Amaranthaceae), which has about 75 genera and 900 species worldwide.

There are about 70 species of amaranth worldwide. Pigweed or redroot (*Amaranthus retroflexus*) is perhaps the most commonly used species here in the United States.

IDENTIFYING AMARANTH

Amaranth plants can be erect or prostrate, and the leaves are alternately arranged on the stems. The lower root or the underside of the lower leaves is often tinted red.

The small, green, and inconspicuous flowers are borne in dense, bristly spikes. They mature to a light brown or tan color, and often give the plant a scruffy appearance. The black or white seeds are formed in dense flower spikes.

Various amaranths are common weeds throughout the United States. The plant seems to prefer disturbed soils.

USES

The leaves and tender stems are mild flavored and are most versatile. When used raw, they make a hearty and filling salad. When simply steamed and seasoned lightly, they are delicious. Your guests will ask for more. The leaves and stems can be chopped and added to omelets, soups, fried vegetables, and sandwiches.

Young amaranth (*Amaranthus retroflexus*). PHOTO BY RICK ADAMS.

A view of the young *Amaranthus retroflexus*. Note the red root. PHOTO BY RICK ADAMS.

The seeds have long been used in food and ceremony. When Cortes arrived in Mexico in 1519, the white-seeded amaranths were as important as corn. With a seed whose protein content was 15 percent and that provided a host of vitamins and minerals, it is no wonder that this drought-resistant and easily cultivated plant played the role it did. These white amaranth seeds held a prominent part in the Indians' religious ceremonies. The small seeds would be mixed with honey—or with blood—and formed into little idols that were carried through the streets and then eaten by the participants. The Christian Spaniards were appalled at what they saw as a combination of paganism, blood worship, and what the priests regarded as a mockery of the Christian Eucharist. The plant was outlawed and the crop was suppressed, becoming nearly extinct.

Today, researchers and gardeners the world over are rediscovering the incredible value of this easily grown, high-protein plant. It is a true survival food that should be in every garden.

The seeds of amaranth are easily harvested by hand. They can be ground (or even used whole) and used in cakes, pancakes, and all bread products. They are good added to soups. The seeds can also be sprouted and added to salads or tostadas.

When collecting leaves and tender stems for food, do not uproot the entire plant and it will continue to put forth new growth for the remainder of the season.

Rick Adams next to one of the tall amaranths, now seeding.

One of the erect amaranths.

Homestead Tostada (Cheese Tostada with Amaranth)

(Use young amaranth leaves as you'd use lettuce)
Oil
1 corn tortilla
¼ cup shredded cheese (your choice, but I prefer swiss)
½ cup amaranth leaves
2 tablespoons salsa

Warm a cast-iron skillet on your fire and add oil. Put in the tortilla and let it get warm for about 3 minutes. Add cheese and let cook until it begins to melt. Chop the amaranth leaves (any variety) well and add them to the skillet. Let tostada cook for another 2 or 3 minutes. Then scoop about 2 tablespoons of salsa over it and serve.

Note: Some amaranth leaves grow bitter as they mature. To test, simply chew on a leaf. If it's too bitter for your palate, use the leaves in a fully cooked recipe instead.

SERVES ONE.

Survival Salad

1 cup amaranth greens
1 cup New Zealand spinach greens
1 cup chickweed greens
½ cup nasturtium leaves
½ cup onions (greens and roots), diced
4 large Jerusalem artichokes, diced
1 lemon
Sprinkle of salt
2 tablespoons chia seeds

Why is this recipe called Survival Salad? Most of these items can be found growing, or can be cultivated, in urban backyards. The onions and Jerusalem artichokes are easily grown; once established, they more or less take care of themselves and will reseed themselves indefinitely. The amaranth, New Zealand spinach, and nasturtium are very easy to get established in your yard. They too will reseed themselves ad infinitum if you make certain that they have well-drained, almost sandy soil and occasional water. The chickweed doesn't need to be cultivated since it can be found growing wild over most of the United States. Chickweed is most abundant in the spring, and it is found in shady areas with moist soil.

If you experience a genuine food crisis, you will be able to provide quality meals without joining the panicked mobs looting the corner market (if you've planned ahead).

Campers can easily prepare a salad like this, needing to carry along only the onion (unless wild ones can be found), Jerusalem artichokes (unless you're in the eastern United States, where they can be found in the wild), lemon, salt, and chia seeds.

Rinse all of the greens and tear them into bite-size pieces. Add the diced onion and the diced Jerusalem artichokes.

For seasoning, squeeze the juice of the lemon (maybe from your backyard lemon tree) over the salad ingredients. If you have no lemons, substitute raw apple cider vinegar. (No vinegar either? I've made a flavorful seasoning by soaking about six fresh white sage leaves—any sage will do though—in ⅓ cup of water until the water is strongly sage flavored. Then I pour the water into the salad.)

Add salt and chia seeds. No salt? Add powdered seaweed or powdered saltbush (*Atriplex* spp.).

Toss the salad well and savor it thoughtfully.

SERVES FIVE.

Little Tokyo Supreme

1 cup amaranth leaves
½ cup tender amaranth stems
½ cup tofu
⅓ cup bean sprouts
3 cups "vegetarian chicken" broth (can use bouillon cubes)

Add the amaranth leaves, stems, tofu, and bean sprouts to the broth and let simmer for about 15 minutes.

For lunch, serve with cottage cheese. For dinner, serve with a baked potato.

SERVES FOUR.

Mrs. Williams' Kalaloo (Stir-Fry Amaranth)

1 tablespoon butter
1 cup amaranth leaves
1 cup tender amaranth stems, diced
1 cup bean sprouts
1 cup onion, diced
1 cup watercress (with stems), diced
1 tablespoon soy sauce

Warm the butter in a wok. (Use a skillet if camping—unless you bring your wok with you.) Add all the remaining ingredients and cook in the wok. Cook only long enough to wilt the leaves and to partially cook the other ingredients; the watercress stems, onion, bean sprouts, and amaranth stems should still have a bit of crunch to them.

Serve with a seasoning of soy sauce.

SERVES FOUR.

Amish Memories (Amaranth Cheese Dish)

2 cups tender amaranth stems and leaves
1½ cups ricotta cheese
⅓ cup Parmesan cheese, grated
2 eggs, beaten

Cook the amaranth by steaming until tender. Chop into bite-size pieces. Combine the amaranth with the cheeses and eggs. Put into a covered casserole dish and bake in a 250°F oven for about 20 to 30 minutes. If you're cooking over a campfire, put the ingredients in a covered pot and suspend the pot about 6 inches from the coals. Approximately 15 minutes of cooking should be sufficient.

SERVES THREE OR FOUR.

Squatters' Paradise (Amaranth Vegetable Dish)

3 cups amaranth leaves and tender stems
1 onion, finely diced
Butter
½ cup walnuts, almonds, or peanuts, chopped fine

Collect the amaranth leaves and the tender stems. Cut them into bite-size pieces and put into a steamer with one finely diced onion. Let steam until it is all tender.

Season each serving with a pat of butter, and then sprinkle the finely chopped nuts over the top.

SERVES THREE.

Arroyo Sunrise (Amaranth and Eggs)

3 cups amaranth leaves and tender stems
Butter
2 hard-boiled eggs, sliced
Dash of paprika

First, make sure the amaranth leaves are still young and not bitter. Clean the amaranth and break into bite-size pieces. Melt a slice of butter in a cast-iron skillet and add the amaranth. (Or instead of butter, use the fat left over from frying bacon.) Let the amaranth cook until it's all wilted.

When cooked, serve the amaranth with slices of hard-boiled eggs and a dash of paprika on top.

SERVES TWO.

Amaranth Power Loaf

1 cup amaranth seeds
1 cup whole-wheat flour or acorn flour
3 teaspoons baking powder
1 teaspoon sea salt
3 tablespoons honey
1 egg
1 cup raw milk (or milk made from powder)
3 tablespoons oil

Collect the amaranth seeds and winnow to remove any foreign matter. Use either the cultivated giant amaranth seeds or any of the wild amaranths. Generally, the cultivated amaranths have white seeds and the wild amaranths have black seeds. They are all used the same, and they do not need to be ground before using in bread recipes. However, the white seeds tend not to be as hard as the black, and the white seeds have a nuttier flavor. The seeds can be soaked in water before baking, but this is not essential.

Combine all the ingredients and mix well. Bake in a greased standard bread pan for about a half-hour at 300°F. If you're cooking over a fire, put your dough in a greased pan and invert another larger pan over the first to create an oven effect. Place the pan on a grill over a bed of hot coals so that the pan is about 6 inches from the coals. This recipe will awaken an instinctive sense in civilized man as he realizes that his refined diet is a very limited fare.

SERVES SIX, DEPENDING ON THICKNESS OF SLICES.

Powerhouse Omelet Pancakes

1 cup amaranth leaves, finely chopped
1 cup onion (wild or cultivated), finely chopped
2 tablespoons chia seeds
3 eggs, beaten
1 teaspoon garlic powder
Oil

Mix all the ingredients together. Warm a skillet with a little oil and spoon out about 3 tablespoons of this mixture per "pancake." Let cook well on one side, flip, and serve when it is "done" enough, per your taste. Great in the morning.

SERVES THREE.

ASPARAGUS, WILD (*Asparagus officinalis*)

Asparagus was formerly classified as a member of the Lily family. Now it is classified in the Asparagus family (Asparagaceae). This family contains three or more genera worldwide, depending on your interpretation, and 320 species worldwide.

The *Asparagus* genus contains about 300 species worldwide.

IDENTIFYING ASPARAGUS

If you've ever seen asparagus in the supermarket, you'll have no trouble recognizing the young spears as they emerge in the spring. There is simply little difference in overall appearance because it's the same plant.

The spears of this European native will, if left uncut, develop into large fern-like plants, often up to 5 feet tall in mature rootstocks. The leaves become intricately branched into needle-like segments, and small bell-shaped light green flowers develop. The flowers are followed by small green berries that eventually mature to red.

USES

Wild asparagus is prepared in the same way that you'd prepare and serve store-bought or garden-grown asparagus. Collect the newly emerging spears in the spring. Don't take all the spears from each root crown each season because that

A view of asparagus.

may kill the root. Leave at least one spear at each root crown to mature and go to seed. As the plants develop and become ferny, they are inedible.

The plant is found throughout the United States in fields, by roadsides, etc.

Asparagus spears can be eaten raw in salads, and they are delicious this way. Some people, however, have reported a mild dermatitis reaction from eating the spears raw.

More commonly, the spears are steamed and eaten with a light seasoning. They can be served with a cream sauce, butter, cheese, or other vegetables. I enjoy my asparagus with hard-boiled eggs.

Wild asparagus spears are identical to asparagus spears sold at the market.

Asparagus is an ideal plant to grow in the garden. As a perennial, it will produce its new spears year after year, with no further plantings, And when it is not the season to collect the young spears, the ferny asparagus plant will grace your garden with beauty.

Saturday Night Asparagus (Steamed Asparagus)

6 thick asparagus spears
Butter

If you're unable to boil asparagus spears, consider "steaming" them in the coals of a campfire. Wrap at least a half-dozen spears in several layers of leaves (such as corn husk, coltsfoot, large mustard leaves, or other leaves that are not toxic) and then wait for your fire to die down to a bed of glowing coals.

Place your asparagus bundle in the coals, making a slight depression in the middle of the coals where the asparagus will nestle. In about 15 minutes or so, turn the wrapped bundle and let it steam inside the leaves for another 15 minutes.

If your timing is right, you'll have some deliciously tender asparagus spears when you open the bundle of leaves. Serve with some butter and enjoy one of nature's finest foods.

SERVES TWO.

Spears on Toast

Asparagus spears
Butter
Mayonnaise
Whole-wheat toast
Chopped chives or finely diced wild onion greens

Steam the asparagus spears until tender. Spread butter and mayonnaise on the whole-wheat toast. Sprinkle diced chives or finely diced wild onion greens over the toast. Place two or three asparagus spears on each slice of toast and serve warm. Simple and delicious!

SERVES ONE.

Ranch Hand Snack (Cream Sauce over Asparagus and Eggs)

About a dozen asparagus spears
4 hard-boiled eggs

SAUCE

⅓ cup butter
½ cup soy flour
1 cup milk (can be made from powdered milk)
1 cup water (use the water from boiling the asparagus)
Dash of pepper

Collect about a dozen tender, plump asparagus spears. Gently boil (or steam) them and then cut into 1-inch segments. Slice the hard-boiled eggs and place them in the same pan as the asparagus. Make a sauce by blending the butter with the flour, and then gradually adding the milk, on a low heat. Stir well so the sauce is not lumpy, and stir in the water and pepper.

The sauce is now poured over the asparagus and eggs and gently folded in. Cover the pan and bake in a 300°F oven for about 20 minutes, until the asparagus and eggs are well heated. If you cook this over the coals of a campfire, be careful not to burn the sauce.

SERVES FOUR.

Oklahoma Summer Salad

2 cups tender asparagus spears
3 hard-boiled eggs, sliced
Several olives
¾ cup watercress, chopped
½ cup chickweed, chopped
½ cup sow thistle leaves, chopped
¼ cup onion leaves, diced
2 tablespoons lemon juice
½ teaspoon salt or kelp pepper
½ teaspoon paprika
½ cup sour cream (if unavailable, add 2 tablespoons salad oil or 3 tablespoons mayonnaise)

Steam or boil two cups of tender asparagus spears. Cut into small pieces. Add the sliced eggs and the olives to the asparagus and chill. (These ingredients can be chilled in a river or other body of water if you're out camping and don't have access to a refrigerator. Put the asparagus, eggs, and olives in a sealed container and place the container in the water.) When chilled, add the watercress, chickweed, and sow thistle and onion leaves, well diced. Make certain that all the leaves are still tender and not bitter. Mix in the lemon juice, salt (or kelp), paprika, and sour cream. Oil can be substituted for sour cream, but the results are not the same.

Toss the salad lightly and serve immediately.

SERVES SIX.

Boiled asparagus with hard-boiled eggs.

Chardon Crepes

2 cups tender asparagus spears
8 pieces whole-wheat bread or sourdough bread
Butter
Sliced meat, such as beef, buffalo, turkey

Cook the tender asparagus spears and cut into approximately 4-inch pieces. Butter the bread and place a thin slice of meat on each piece. Then place several asparagus spears on each piece of bread. This can now be served as an open-faced sandwich, or you can make crepes. Roll the bread around the meat and asparagus and secure the ends with toothpicks. Place the crepes in a skillet or in a covered baking dish and cook at a low temperature until warm.

SERVES FOUR.

Savory Summer Soup

2 cups tender asparagus spears
6 cups chicken stock (or use vegetarian bouillon cubes)
½ cup celery, chopped
½ cup onion bulb and leaves (wild or homegrown), chopped
3 tablespoons butter
3 tablespoons flour (whole-wheat or potato)
½ cup cream (or use milk; made from powder is okay)
¼ teaspoon paprika
¼ teaspoon sea salt
¼ teaspoon pepper
Hard-boiled eggs, sliced, for garnish

Cut the asparagus spears into pieces and simmer in the chicken stock. Add the chopped celery and onion and cover pan. In a small bowl, blend the butter and flour into a fine paste, and gradually add the cream to form an even consistency. Add the seasoning, then mix this mixture into the soup stock, stirring while you add. Cover again and simmer for about ½ hour before serving.

Serve with hard-boiled egg slices.

SERVES ABOUT SIX.

BRACKEN (*Pteridium aquilinum*)

Bracken is a member of the Bracken family (Dennstaedtiaceae). This family has 11 genera and about 170 species worldwide.

The *Pteridium* genus is believed to consist of about five species worldwide.

IDENTIFYING BRACKEN FERN

These ferns usually have solitary stalks and dark, cord-like creeping rootstocks. The plants can grow from 1 to 4 feet high, and the fronds are twice-pinnately divided. The spore-bearing cases (called sori) are found in lines along the margins of the mature fronds. The young shoots are the edible portion, and they have the appearance of the head of a fiddle, hence the common name "fiddlehead."

Bracken fern is found throughout the entire United States, usually in moist, rich woods.

Young bracken. PHOTO BY RICK ADAMS.

An ideal bracken "fiddlehead." PHOTO BY BARBARA KOLANDER.

A view of the mature bracken frond. PHOTO BY RICK ADAMS.

USES

Young uncurling bracken fronds, commonly called fiddleheads, have long been a favorite of many people. The fiddleheads are pinched off, sometimes wiped of any outer layer of fibrous hairs, and cooked in a variety of ways. The simplest method is to steam the fiddleheads and serve with butter, or various sauces.

Mature fern fronds are not eaten—especially not raw—since some may be toxic.

Bracken fiddleheads. PHOTO BY BARBARA KOLANDER.

Generally speaking, the young uncurling fiddleheads of all ferns can be pinched off and eaten, once cooked. I have eaten the bracken fiddleheads raw in salads and the flavor was distinctly nutty. You can safely eat all young fiddleheads from all ferns.

If you are uncertain that you have bracken, it would be best to cook the fiddleheads before eating. Also keep the following principle always in the forefront of your thinking while foraging: When in doubt, do without.

There have been some suggestions that fiddleheads should be eaten with caution, based on the fact that fiddleheads contain a substance called ptaquiloside. Japanese consider wild fiddleheads one of the great foods of spring, and Native Americans have used fiddleheads for food for centuries. It turns out that both of these groups have a higher incidence of intestinal cancer, which could be linked to the ingestion of fiddleheads. But since the hard data is both lacking and inconclusive, the cancer could be from something else.

Many wild food foragers regard fiddleheads, which are usually just eaten in moderation in the spring, as a safe food. As with all such things in life, you should proceed with caution, and continue to do research. And don't let your preferences and opinions get in the way of hard facts when you discover new data.

Fit and Fiddle (a Traditional Fiddlehead Dish)

2 cups young fiddleheads
Butter
Garlic powder

Steam (or boil lightly) the fiddleheads in a covered container for about 5 minutes. Season with butter and garlic powder, if available. Even simply steamed and served, this is a favorite vegetable for many people.

SERVES FOUR.

Fiddle de Dum

2 cups young fiddleheads
⅓ stick butter
⅓ cup whole-wheat crackers, crushed
1 lemon
Powdered herbal seasoning (such as Spike)

Steam or boil the young fiddleheads until tender. Warm the butter and combine it with the crushed whole-wheat crackers. Sprinkle the crackers and butter over the cooked fiddleheads before serving. Season to taste with lemon and the herbal seasoning.

SERVES FOUR.

Big Bear Bracken (a Cream Sauce Dish)

2 cups young fiddleheads

CREAM SAUCE

2 tablespoons butter
2 tablespoons whole-wheat flour
1 cup cream (or milk, from powder is acceptable)

Collect, clean, and steam 2 cups of young bracken fiddleheads. While they are steaming, melt 2 tablespoons of butter in a saucepan and stir in the flour. Slowly add the cream, continually stirring so no lumps form. Do not boil—cook at a very low temperature. If desired, add a dash of salt and pepper.

Serve by dividing the cooked fiddleheads into individual dishes. Pour the warm cream sauce over the fiddleheads and serve immediately.

This was a favorite method of preparation by wild food educator Barbara Kolander.

SERVES THREE OR FOUR.

Hollandaise Holiday

2 cups fiddleheads

Steam the fiddleheads until tender. Serve with either of the following sauces, which aren't "real" hollandaise, but simpler, mock versions.

MOCK HOLLANDAISE SAUCE I

2 beaten eggs
¼ cup cream
¼ teaspoon salt or kelp
¼ teaspoon paprika
1 tablespoon lemon juice
2 tablespoons butter

Cook and stir all the ingredients (except the butter) at low heat in a saucepan until they become thick. When thick, add the butter, a little at a time. Pour the sauce over the bracken and serve at once.

MOCK HOLLANDAISE SAUCE II

1 cup sour cream
Juice of 1 lemon
2 egg yolks (Don't throw away the whites! Save them for a breakfast omelet or for soup. If nothing else, add the whites to your dog's breakfast, or use the whites as a hair conditioner—but don't throw them away!)
½ teaspoon salt
½ teaspoon paprika

Stir all the ingredients at very low heat until thick. Pour over bracken and serve.

Both sauces are best made in a double boiler (with boiling water in the bottom half). However, if you don't have a double boiler, simply use a stainless-steel skillet, cook at a very low heat, and stir continuously.

SERVES FOUR.

BURDOCK (*Arctium minus*)

There are 10 species of *Arctium* throughout Europe, with two species being common in the United States.

IDENTIFYING BURDOCK

Wild burdock is found throughout most of the United States. The first time I saw wild burdock, I thought I was looking at a rhubarb plant, though the stalk was not red and celery-like, as with rhubarb.

The first-year plant produces a rosette of rhubarb-type leaves; in ideal soil, the second-year plant produces a stalk 6 to 9 feet tall. Both species are similar, with *Arctium lappa* growing a bit taller than *Arctium minus*.

The leaves are heart shaped (cordate) or broadly ovate, and are conspicuously veined. The first-year leaves are large and up to 2 feet in length. In the second season, the plant sends up a flower stalk with similar, but smaller, leaves. The purple to white flowers, compressed in bur-like heads, bloom in July and August. The seed containers are spiny-hooked burs that stick to socks and pants.

Burdock's root looks like an elongated carrot, except that it is white inside with a brownish-gray skin that is peeled away before eating. You sometimes find cultivated versions of this root in the markets sold as "gobo."

A burdock leaf

The first-year burdock leaf. PHOTO BY LOUIS-M. LANDRY.

The burdock seed clusters. PHOTO BY JEAN PAWEK.

The burdock root is cleaned, and peeled if necessary. The root is sliced and ready for cooking.

USES

The first-year roots can be dug, washed, and eaten once peeled. They are usually simmered in water until tender and cooked with other vegetables. In Russia, the roots have been used as potato substitutes when potatoes aren't available. The texture and flavor of boiled burdock roots is unique, though it does resemble a potato. The roots can also be peeled and sliced into thin pieces and sautéed or cooked with vegetables. I also eat young, tender roots diced into salad, and I find them very tasty.

Leaves can be eaten once boiled; in some cases, two boilings are necessary, depending on your taste. Try to get them very young. Peeled leaf stems can be eaten raw or cooked. The erect flower stalks, collected before the flowers open, can be peeled of their bitter green skin and then dried or cooked, though these tend to be much more fibrous than the leaf stems.

An analysis of the root (100 grams or ½ cup) shows 50 mg of calcium, 58 mg of phosphorus, and 180 mg of potassium. Tea of the roots is said to be useful in treating rheumatism.

Herbalists all over the world use burdock: The roots and seeds are a soothing demulcent, tonic, and alterative (restorative to normal health).

You can also take the large burdock leaves and wrap fish and game in them before roasting in the coals of a fire pit. Foods cooked this way are mildly seasoned by the leaves.

CATTAIL (*Typha* spp.)

Cattails are members of the Cattail family (Typhaceae), which contains two genera and about 32 species worldwide.

The *Typha* genus contains about 15 species worldwide.

IDENTIFYING CATTAIL

All members of *Typha*—all cattails—are similarly recognized and used similarly. These are inhabitants of swamps, riversides, back bays, ditches, and other wet places. The long, grass-like leaves can rise to 6 feet and taller. The flowering spike is most conspicuous and easily recognized as the brown "hot-dog-on-a-stick" that is so commonly used in dried floral arrangements.

USES

Cattail has been called the supermarket of the swamps because it yields so many foods and useful items.

The conspicuous brown flowering spike of autumn is edible but not when it is brown. You must collect it in the early spring while it is still green. These green spikes are boiled and served like corn on the cob, tasting remarkably similar to corn. The uppermost part of the flowering spike is full of a fine yellow pollen. This pollen can be collected by bending the spikes into a paper bag, shaking to remove the pollen, and then releasing the spike. The pollen is then sifted and used with other flours for cooking pastry products.

Before the cattail plant has flowered, the inside of the shoot is tender and edible. The shoot should first be squeezed toward the bottom of the shoot to

Angelo Cervera shows the just-picked green cattail spikes, ready to be boiled and buttered.

Cattail spikes are eaten when they are young and green. PHOTO BY RICK ADAMS.

make certain it is not too fibrous to eat. If it's still tender, briskly pull up the shoot. Peel back the fibrous, green outer leaves. The lower section of the shoot—about 12 inches—is usually the most tender. It can be eaten raw in salads or cooked by steaming or adding to soups.

Underground, where the fibrous rhizomes meet the shoot, there is an approximately golf ball–size piece of carbohydrate material. It is directly underneath each shoot and must be gathered before the cattail flowers or it will become too fibrous to eat. This starchy lump is sometimes erroneously called a tuber, and sometimes it is called the "cattail potato." This part of the cattail is first peeled

The long leaves and the mature brown flower spikes of the cattail. The flower spikes are not edible in this stage.

The young shoots of the cattail, being prepared for a meal. The green outer leaves—which are more fibrous—are first removed.

of its slightly fibrous rind and is then used raw in salads or exactly as you'd use potatoes.

Also arising from the rhizomes are small white "baby" shoots. They are usually found beneath the water or mud, and they are simply the very young shoots. These small shoots can be easily pinched off and eaten raw in salads or cooked in soups or vegetable dishes.

Cattail is an important food item that also yields many other useful products. Chopsticks can be made from the tough flower stalks. The leaves can be dried, moistened, and woven into sandals, mats, baskets, etc. The dried brown spikes make excellent torches when dipped in oil or tallow; when the brown spikes are broken open, the down-like filaments attached to each seed are released. This down-like material is excellent as tinder for fire-starting, for an insulating material, or for pressing into minor wounds to stop the bleeding.

Big Bend Breakfast

Approximately 12 young cattail shoots
½ cup shredded swiss cheese

Collect about one dozen tender young cattail shoots. Peel off the outer fibrous layers—usually all the green layers are too fibrous to eat and should be removed. You'll be able to eat the bottom 12 inches (or so) of each shoot. To determine how much you can use, bite into the peeled shoot. If it is too fibrous, cut off another inch or two and test again.

Once they are rinsed, gently boil the shoots in plain water for 5 minutes. Drain off the water and (using the same pan, or a different pan with a lid) shred cheese over the cattail shoots. Cover the pan and return to the fire with a very low heat. About 2 minutes is sufficient to melt the cheese.

Serve immediately.

SERVES THREE.

Cossack Asparagus

Approximately 12 tender cattail shoots
Butter
Kelp powder

Collect the tender young shoots of cattail before they become fibrous. Use the portion of the shoot above the rhizome for about 12 inches or so. Peel back the fibrous green layers until you are left with a tender white shoot.

Cut these shoots into 1-inch segments, and then boil or steam for about 5 minutes. Serve with a dab of butter and a shake of kelp powder. This is a delicious vegetable, but it is only available in late winter and spring before the shoots become fibrous.

SERVES FOUR.

Baby Whites

¼ onion, sliced
About 20 baby white cattail shoots, before they've started to become green and slightly fibrous
2 cups watercress, chopped

Begin by gently cooking the sliced onion in a cast-iron skillet. When they are about half cooked, add about 20 of the baby white shoots, cleaned of any soil. It is not necessary to slice the shoots. Wait about 5 minutes and add the watercress. Cover the skillet and let cook until the watercress is well steamed.

Seasoning is not necessary, although a dash of garlic salt can be added.

SERVES THREE.

Treestump Special

5 cups young cattail shoots and the starchy bases of each shoot
1 carrot, diced
2 cloves garlic
½ cup lamb's-quarters greens, chopped
4 cups water
½ cup whole-wheat flour
2 tablespoons kelp powder

Collect and clean 5 cups of the tender cattail shoots and the starchy bulb-like base of each shoot. Dice the shoots and bulb-like bases and put them into a soup pot with the diced carrot and the garlic cloves (diced or whole). Add the lamb's-quarters greens and the water, then let the mixture simmer. When the ingredients look about half-cooked, make a sauce with the wheat flour. Put the flour and kelp into a cup and add water, a little at a time, and stir until you get a fine sauce. Slowly pour this into the stew, while stirring. Let the stew cook for another 15 to 20 minutes before serving.

This is an easily made stew, and any wild greens in season can be used if lamb's-quarters leaves are unavailable.

SERVES SIX.

Pleasant Street Illinois

10 tender cattail shoots
½ red onion (or ⅓ cup wild onion)
½ cup chickweed
1 tablespoon olive oil
1 tablespoon apple cider vinegar
Squeeze of lemon
Kelp powder and powdered dill weed to taste
1 ripe avocado, 1 tomato (optional)

Pull up the still-tender cattail shoots, and peel back all the green fibrous outer layers. Use the lower part of the stalk that is white and tender, about the lower 12 inches or so. Dice the shoots into thin segments. Finely dice ½ of a red onion (or ⅓ cup of wild onion). Add ½ cup of chickweed greens, torn into bite-size pieces. The chickweed can be substituted for ½ cup of young watercress, chopped into bite-size pieces. (Watercress is commonly found growing near cattails.) Season the salad with the oil, vinegar, lemon, and the powdered kelp and dill. Mix well. Add an avocado or tomato if you wish.

MAKES FOUR MEDIUM SERVINGS.

Cayahuga Chips

Two cups of the starchy "bulbs" found at the base of each cattail shoot and above the rhizome
Vegetable oil

Collect the starchy, roundish part of the cattail (found at the base of each shoot) by carefully pulling up a young and tender nonflowering plant and cutting off the rhizome and the actual shoot. The resultant "bulb" (not botanically a bulb) will then need to be peeled of an outer layer, leaving an edible portion generally a bit smaller than a golf ball.

Wash the "bulbs," slice thin, and fry in vegetable oil. Lightly salt these chips (if desired) and serve warm.

SERVES FOUR.

Cat on the Cob

6 green cattail spikes
Water
Butter

Collect the still-green cattail spikes of spring. These are the flowering spikes that turn brown in autumn.

Steam or boil them in a covered pan for about 10 minutes. When done, drain the water and serve the green spikes with butter.

Eat them like corn on the cob.

SERVES TWO.

Kansas Casserole

2 cups green flower spike material, scraped from the flower spikes
½ cup rice, cooked
½ cup soybeans, cooked and mashed
1 egg
½ cup milk (you can use powdered milk)
2 tablespoons oil
1 garlic clove, finely chopped
Kelp powder, to taste

When the cattail flower spikes are still green, collect several of them and scrape off the green material, leaving only the bare stalk. To this green spike material add ½ cup of cooked rice and ½ cup of cooked and mashed soybeans. Add 1 egg, ½ cup of milk, oil, finely chopped garlic clove, and kelp to taste. Mix this together well in a covered casserole dish and bake at 250°F for about 30 minutes. If you're cooking over a campfire, place the covered pot on a grill about 6 inches above your campfire coals. It should be well cooked in about 30 minutes.

One cup of dried bread crumbs can be used in place of the rice and soybeans.

Cattail Pollen

Use it like flour.

Collect the pollen from the top of each cattail spike by bending the flower spike into a brown paper bag and shaking the spike for a few seconds. This is done in the spring before the seed spike turns brown. Once you've collected a few cups of this fine, yellow pollen (it may take about 100 cattails to get a cup of pollen), sift it to remove foreign material, such as twigs or insects. (Come to think of it, you may want to leave the insects for added protein.)

This yellow pollen can then be used as either an extender or a substitute for regular whole-wheat flour. If wheat flour is available, mix the cattail pollen half and half with it. The cattail pollen is sweet and it adds a yellow color to whatever food it is mixed with.

The pollen is also useful as a thickener for soups, stews, or broths.

Richard's Repast (Yellow Pollen Pancakes)

1 cup yellow cattail pollen
1 cup whole-wheat, rice, or acorn flour
1 teaspoon baking soda
½ teaspoon sea salt
1 tablespoon honey
2 tablespoons oil
2½ cups milk (you can use powdered milk)

Collect the yellow cattail pollen from the top of each cattail flower spike. Sift it to remove any foreign particles. Put the cattail pollen, flour, and all the other ingredients in a large mixing bowl. Beat with a fork until fluffy.

You could also buy a whole-grain pancake mix, and blend an equal part of the mix with an equal part of cattail pollen. Then prepare the pancakes as directed.

Bake the pancakes on an oiled and heated frying pan or pancake griddle. (You can try baking them on a flat hot rock, if nothing else is available. Support the flat rock on other rocks, and build a fire underneath. Be sure to oil the rock first.) Use ripe, crushed berries for a topping. If fresh berries are unavailable, try a topping made from equal parts maple syrup, honey, and blackstrap molasses.

SERVES THREE.

CHICKWEED (*Stellaria media*)

Chickweed is a member of the Pink family (Caryophyllaceae), a family that has 83 to 89 genera and 3,000 species worldwide.

The *Stellaria* genus has 190 species worldwide.

IDENTIFYING CHICKWEED

Chickweed is a low-growing plant with a weak stem. The leaves are opposite and come to a sharp point. The stem has a characteristic line of hairs that can be observed if you look closely. The flowers are white and five-petaled. Each petal has a deep notch, so it appears that there are 10 petals. It grows all across the United States and Europe.

A mildly toxic plant named spurge can be confused with chickweed. However, spurge lacks the white flower (its flower is an inconspicuous green color), and the leaf tips are not pointed, but rounded. Most noticeable is the white sap that exudes from the stem of spurge when broken. Chickweed has no such white sap.

USES

This delicate annual weed is most abundant in spring and early summer. It is a widespread weed, and myopic gardeners typically detest this persistent "volunteer"; they resort to any number of specialized poisons to kill off this gentle creature. Even if these gardeners can't be convinced to include chickweed in their salads, why poison the soil? A far better solution would be to pull up the chickweed and feed it to chickens, rabbits, goats; if you don't raise animals, at least the chickweed can be composted.

Young chickweed.

Chickweed can be used as a steamed vegetable, but it is at its best when served raw. Use it just as you'd use lettuce. Put chickweed in salads, on sandwiches, on tostadas, etc.

The flavor is mild and the texture (when gathered before it gets too old) is tender.

A field of dreams . . . that is, a field of chickweed. PHOTO BY RICK ADAMS.

The author shows students how to identify chickweed for salad. PHOTO BY RICK ADAMS.

Chickweed   53

When collecting, gently tear or cut a handful of this plant, which often grows in dense patches. You don't need to uproot it. Remember, you want to leave some of the plant to go to seed for next year's wild crop. Also, if you simply cut off as much of the stems as you intend to use, the plant will continue to grow, and in some cases it will sprout multiple stems where you cut it.

Pilgrim's Salad

4 cups fresh chickweed
½ onion, diced
Apple cider vinegar and oil dressing

Collect the tender plants and rinse in cold water. Place on your cutting board and cut into smaller bite-size pieces. Put the chickweed into your salad bowl and add ½ of a diced onion or ½ cup of diced wild onion greens. Season with a simple dressing of equal parts apple cider vinegar and olive oil. To enhance the subtle flavor of chickweed, you can add a dash of dill weed and kelp.

SERVES FOUR.

The David Ashley Special (a Salad)

5 cups fresh-picked chickweed, rinsed and torn into bite-size pieces
1 ripe avocado
½ red onion
1 ripe tomato
1 young prickly pear cactus pad, peeled and diced
3 or 4 young fennel stalks, diced
½ cup lamb's-quarters greens, torn into bite-size pieces
1 lemon
2 tablespoons olive oil
1 garlic clove, diced fine
¼ teaspoon sea salt

Combine all the ingredients in a large salad bowl. The avocado, onion, and tomato should be cut into bite-size pieces. Mix it well and serve. Fresh chickweed is not strongly flavored like many other greens, but it has a vibrantly alive flavor.

If you want to introduce your family to wild foods *gradually* by serving only those wild plants that you know they'll enjoy, then begin with chickweed in all your salads. It's refreshing, delicious, and nutritious.

SERVES EIGHT.

Freshly collected chickweed that has been rinsed, ready to be made into a large salad.

Chickweed Royale

3 cups freshly gathered chickweed
½ cup nasturtium leaves and stems
¼ cup garden chives (collect from your herb garden)
2 garlic cloves
¼ teaspoon salt
½ teaspoon powdered sage
2 tablespoons safflower oil
2 tablespoons apple cider vinegar

This is a delicious salad. We made this one in late winter, collecting the greens from a residential backyard in the city of Los Angeles. The wonderful chickweed was gathered from a thick patch of the plant that has been reseeding itself for years in an old garden patch. Likewise, the nasturtium leaves were collected from a plant gone wild that reseeds itself under the shade of the trees. Even the chives were not from an active garden. Planted years before, they now give forth tasty offerings year after year with no care or need for human intervention. Ah! Think of it! Such "wild" gardens could easily be encouraged in all backyards and vacant lots across all lands. A greater measure of self-reliance is truly within our grasp . . .

Back to the recipe. Collect the chickweed and nasturtium not as a thief in the night, but in full appreciation of the bounty that these floral treasures provide. Rinse them, then cut into bite-size pieces. Chop the chives and mince the garlic. Add the seasoning ingredients to the salad and toss well.

We served this vibrant green salad with lentil soup and tuna-soy burgers.

SERVES SEVEN.

Welcome to New York (a Chickweed Stew)

2½ quarts fresh chickweed (use the entire above-ground plant, and cut it all into bite-size segments)
4 large Jerusalem artichokes
½ onion, diced
2 carrots, cut into round slices
2 garlic cloves
3 bay leaves
2 cups water
1 cup New Zealand spinach leaves
½ teaspoon salt
½ teaspoon pepper

Begin by simmering the Jerusalem artichokes, onion, carrots, garlic, and bay leaves in water in a covered pot. Add the rest of the ingredients in about 15 to 20 minutes, when the Jerusalem artichokes and carrots are almost tender. Potatoes can be substituted for the Jerusalem artichokes.

Serve this stew-like dish with a piece of buttered whole-wheat toast.

MAKES THREE OR FOUR MODERATE SERVINGS.

Savory Southwest Sustenance (Simple Chickweed Quesadilla)

Oil
1 corn tortilla
About ⅓ cup shredded cheese (jack or cheddar)
Garlic powder
1 cup fresh chickweed
Salsa

Put the oil in your cast-iron skillet and heat the pan. Add the corn tortilla and cook for about 2 minutes. Add the cheese and let cook at a low heat until the cheese is melted. Sprinkle the garlic powder over the cheese and remove from the skillet. Add rinsed, drained, and chopped chickweed to the top of the quesadilla. Add salsa and serve.

SERVES ONE.

Chrisptado Fantastico (Chickweed Tostada)

1 corn tortilla
Oil
1 egg
¼ cup onion greens, diced
⅓ cup cheddar or jack cheese, shredded
⅓ avocado, sliced
½ tomato, diced
1 teaspoon garlic powder
1 tablespoon alfalfa or chia seed sprouts
1 cup fresh chickweed, rinsed, drained, and chopped
Heaping tablespoon sour cream
Hot salsa, to taste

This is a delicious tostada. Many people have told me that a chickweed tostada is one of their favorite ways to serve chickweed. Indeed, chickweed is delicious substituted for lettuce wherever possible. Of course, this is a highly versatile recipe, but at least try this one if you can. Then feel free to improvise, just as you might do with the lettuce, tomatoes, etc. of a regular tostada.

A tostada of a corn tortilla, cheese, egg, avocado, hot sauce, and chickweed is great. In fact, you can make a fairly good tostada using any one of those three main ingredients (avocado, cheese, egg), hot sauce, and chickweed.

When I make this dish, I first heat the tortilla with a little oil in my cast-iron skillet. I add one egg and cook at a low temperature. When the egg is nearly cooked, I add the diced onions and shredded cheese. When the cheese is melted, I remove the tostada from the pan.

On top of the tostada, I place avocado slices and diced tomato. Next, I sprinkle garlic powder on top, then add the sprouts and chickweed. Finally, I usually place a heaping tablespoon of sour cream on top of the tostada, and add hot salsa to taste.

Serve with a jalapeño pepper or a pickled kelp bladder.

Our friend Suzie Beale was often at our home when I was making this dish, and she coined the unusual name.

SERVES ONE (BUT TWO CAN SPLIT IT).

Young chickweed in flower.

Sedona Sunrise (Steamed Chickweed)

4 cups fresh chickweed
1 cup strongly flavored wild greens (e.g, watercress, radish leaf, dock)
Butter

Clean all the greens you'll be using and then rinse them. Steam them until tender and serve with a pat of butter for seasoning. If you do not have a steamer, gently boil the greens in a minimal amount of water.

SERVES TWO.

Traveler's Loaf

1 slice whole-wheat pita bread (hollow)
3 slices cheese (jack)
⅓ avocado, sliced
4 or 5 thin slices stick salami
½ cup fresh chickweed, rinsed, drained, and chopped
2 thin slices onion bulb (or about ⅓ cup of finely diced wild onion bulbs and leaves—all fibrous parts removed)
Salt to taste

This is an excellent sandwich made from ingredients that are easily carried in a pack, plus chickweed. I've made many lunches with variations of this basic recipe while backpacking.

Cut open a side of the hollow pita bread. Into the cavity, add the cheese slices (even string cheese is good), the avocado slices, and the salami slices. Evenly distribute about ½ cup of fresh, tender chickweed inside the bread, and add the onion slices. Season with a dash of salt and you're ready for lunch.

Find a comfortable tree stump or rock, relax, and enjoy this wonderful "traveler's loaf."

CAN SERVE ONE OR TWO.

CHICORY (*Cichorium intybus*)

Chicory is a member of the Sunflower family. The Sunflower family (Asteraceae) has about 1,500 genera and about 23,000 species. This is one of the largest botanical families. Botanist Willis Linn Jepson divides this very large family into 14 groups. All plants addressed here from the Sunflower family are within "Group 8" (the Chicory Tribe), described as having ligulate heads, five-lobed ligules (five teeth per petal), and generally containing milky sap when broken.

The *Cichorium* genus has only six species.

IDENTIFYING CHICORY

Chicory can grow up to 6 feet tall, though usually it rises about 3 to 4 feet tall. The sky-blue flowers are formed in heads and appear in the upper axils of the plant. Each petal has a ragged edge, caused by the (usually) five teeth on each petal.

The leaves are dandelion-like, but generally much longer and not as toothed. The basal leaves are the longest and are lanceolate in outline. The upper leaves clasp the stem and are similar. The leaves and stalk exude a milky juice when cut. The taproot is the approximate size and shape of a small carrot and tan colored.

USES

Chicory is most famous for its roots, which yield a coffee substitute or coffee extender. The roots can also be cooked and eaten like parsnips.

Chicory roots that have been cultivated.

Aiden Ruiz next to a chicory growing along the tracks. PHOTO BY RICK ADAMS.

The leaves are suitable for use in salads when they are collected early in the spring, before they have become bitter. All the leaves, even the older ones, can be used as cooked greens, either alone or with other leaves.

The plant is a common weed throughout the United States. If you don't have any growing in your yard, it is easy to get a "wild" patch established. Dig up a

A view of the leaves and stem of the chicory plant. PHOTO BY RICK ADAMS.

A close-up of a chicory flower. PHOTO BY RICK ADAMS.

A view of the chicory leaf. PHOTO BY RICK ADAMS.

Chicory plants in flower. PHOTO BY RICK ADAMS.

few roots from the wild and plant them in your yard. Or you can easily order seeds for chicory. Chicory can survive in most soils, but it will do best with full sun and a rich, loamy soil.

Back to the Roots (a Stew)

6 large chicory roots
1 Jerusalem artichoke
1 large gobo (burdock) root
1 medium-sized red potato
1 carrot
1 turnip
1 teaspoon of powdered herbal seasoning (such as Spike)

Gather and clean the chicory roots of all adhering soil. Slice the roots into 1-inch segments and put into your stew pot. Quarter one cleaned Jerusalem artichoke and add the chicory. Wash and slice the gobo root and add to the pot. Clean the potato (no, you don't need to peel it), carrot, and turnip and dice them into small pieces. Add all to the stew pot. Add just enough water to cover the roots. Let simmer, covered, until all the roots are tender. The herbal seasoning can be added to the stew while it cooks, or you can sprinkle it on the roots when serving.

SERVES FOUR OR FIVE.

Get Up and Go Salad

4 cups young, tender chicory leaves
2 cups thinly sliced beets (roots)

DRESSING

2 tablespoons salad oil
2 tablespoons apple cider vinegar
1 tablespoon lemon juice
½ teaspoon salt
½ teaspoon pepper
½ cup watercress leaves and stems, finely minced

Collect the chicory leaves and be certain they are not already bitter. Rinse and tear into bite-size pieces. Add the sliced beets. Mix all the dressing ingredients together by putting into a closed container and shaking well. Pour over the salad and toss lightly. Enjoy.

SERVES FOUR.

Hickory Chicory Dock

2 cups young chicory leaves
2 cups dock greens
1 cup hickory nut meats, minced
2 tablespoons butter

This is one of those recipes that we just had to concoct and try. You'll enjoy eating it, and you'll enjoy talking about it even more.

Taste the chicory leaves to be certain that they are not too old and bitter. If they are exceedingly bitter, first drop them into boiling water, and then drain the water after about 5 minutes. Now use them in the following recipe.

Steam (or gently cook in a small amount of water) 2 cups each of chicory and dock leaves, torn into bite-size pieces. Before serving, sprinkle minced hickory nuts over the cooked greens and add the butter. Add a dash of salt if desired. Minced walnuts, almonds, or peanuts can be used if hickory nuts are unavailable.

SERVES THREE.

Trinity Salad

1 cup tender young chicory leaves (not yet bitter)
1 cup tender chickweed, rinsed
1 cup black mustard leaves
¼ cup mustard flowers and unopened flower buds
1 tomato, diced
½ red onion, diced
1 teaspoon dill weed, powdered
1 tablespoon olive oil
1 tablespoon apple cider vinegar
1 teaspoon pepper
1 teaspoon powdered kelp

Taste the chicory greens to be sure they haven't yet become bitter. Collect a cup each of chicory, chickweed, and mustard leaves. Tear them into small pieces and put in your salad bowl. Add the mustard flowers and unopened buds and the diced tomato. Add the diced red onion, or approximately ⅓ to ½ cup of diced wild onions (bulbs and leaves, removing any fibrous parts) and add to salad. Add all the dressing ingredients to the salad bowl, gently toss, and serve.

SERVES FIVE.

Country Chicory Fry

Bacon fat
2 cups young chicory leaves
½ onion

Using the grease from fried bacon, oil a skillet and warm it. Rinse the chicory and tear it into bite-size pieces. (Older chicory may be extremely bitter; in this case, first drop the chicory leaves into boiling water. Let cook for no more than 5 minutes. Remove the leaves and use in this recipe.) Dice the onion and put it into the skillet and lightly sauté. Add the chicory and cook until wilted. Serve warm.

SERVES TWO.

Chicory Brew

The washed, dried, ground, roasted, and percolated roots of chicory have long been used as a coffee extender and as a caffeine-free coffee substitute. Although the use of chicory has traditionally been associated with poverty, it appears that there are health benefits from drinking chicory. Keeping the liver decongested is a key to good health, according to the herbalist Gene Matlock, and "the herb for liver congestion is chicory." Matlock states that habitual coffee drinking congests the liver to the point that it almost ceases to function. It is no wonder, says Matlock, that Southerners and Latin Americans (who drink much coffee to overcome the "lazy heat") add chicory to their coffee. The origin of adding chicory to coffee is not, according to Matlock, due to poverty;

Gary Gonzales with a can of chicory coffee.

rather, it is to counteract certain physical effects of coffee. Herbalists recognize chicory as a diuretic, laxative, and hepatic.

When collecting roots to make this brew, collect only the largest roots, leaving the smaller ones for reproduction. Wash the roots of all remaining soil and then dry them in an oven, in the sun, or over the coals of a fire. When bone-dry, grind the roots to a powder. This powder is then roasted (in the oven or over coals) until it is deep brown (coffee-colored). Be careful not to burn the powder! The roasted powder is now ready to be mixed with coffee (generally half and half) or used alone and percolated. Drink black or flavor with a spoonful of unfiltered, uncooked honey and a bit of cream.

DANDELION (*Taraxacum officinale*)

Dandelion is a member of the Sunflower family (Asteraceae). The Sunflower family has about 1,500 genera and about 23,000 species. This is one of the largest botanical families in the world. Jepson divides this very large family into 14 groups. All plants addressed here from the Sunflower family are within "Group 8" (the Chicory Tribe), described as having ligulate heads, five-lobed ligules (five teeth per petal), and generally containing milky sap when broken.

The *Taraxacum* genus contains 60 species worldwide.

IDENTIFYING DANDELION

Most of us can identify dandelion on sight since we have observed it since childhood.

The plant produces heads of yellow flowers on leafless stalks each spring. The flowers then mature into cottony balls of winged seeds.

The leaves are all basal and toothed. The plant is a perennial, producing new leaves from the same root year after year.

The dandelion rosette of toothed leaves and the single yellow flower that appears on a leafless stalk.

The beautiful dandelion flower.

A healthy patch of dandelions going to seed.

The root of dandelion.

A dandelion growing next to a rock.

The dandelion root, crown, and leaves can all be utilized.

Foraging Wild Edible Plants of North America

USES

Dandelion, a European native, is perhaps one of America's best-known weeds. It is the common inhabitant of lawns and fields. The leaves are all basal and low-growing, so the plant is most recognized when the colorful yellow spring flowers poke their heads above the surrounding grass.

Dandelion's claim to fame seems to be the wine that so many winemakers produce each spring. This wine was immortalized by Ray Bradbury's classic *Dandelion Wine*—a novel of childhood and childhood dreams.

During hard times and good, countless people have used the tender young spring greens for salad or cooked greens.

Even the roots are used, just like chicory, for a type of caffeine-free coffee substitute or coffee extender. The roots can also be steamed or stewed and eaten.

Between the root and the leaves is a section called the crown. This vegetable is stewed, fried, simmered, steamed, and generally used as a most versatile vegetable in many dishes.

Many children have earned money on the weekends by pulling dandelions from a neighbor's lawn. (My father used to pay me a nickel a root when I was five or six, before I knew about eating the roots.) Children also enjoy blowing away the mature seed ball of the dandelion and making a wish.

We should not be distressed when we see a lawn full of dandelions; we should smile. We should feel that there is still hope for the world.

Golden Sunrise (a Salad)

3 cups very young dandelion greens
3 cups chickweed
½ red onion, diced
1 hard-boiled egg, sliced
2 tablespoons peanut oil
2 tablespoons apple cider vinegar
Salt and pepper, to taste

Taste the dandelion leaves before you gather them for salad. They become bitter quickly, so unless you're collecting the very youngest spring growth, you may prefer using the dandelion greens cooked. If the leaves are not yet bitter, collect about 3 cups of the leaves. Collect about 3 cups of chickweed leaves also. Rinse the leaves, tear them into bite-size pieces, and put them all into your salad bowl. Add the diced onion, the hard-boiled egg slices, and season with the oil, vinegar, and salt and pepper to taste.

Toss the salad well and serve this spring tonic as a lunch or dinner salad.

SERVES ABOUT FIVE.

Lion's Tooth Delight

2 cups cleaned dandelion leaves
1 cup dandelion crowns
Olive oil
½ onion, diced
Garlic powder
Slice of butter

Collect 2 cups of the young dandelion leaves and rinse them well. Also collect 1 cup of the crowns—the section where the root and leaves meet. Warm a cast-iron skillet with oil and add the diced onions. Let cook for about 3 minutes and then add the crowns. Continue cooking until the onions and crowns are almost tender. Add the dandelion leaves and cook until all is done.

Serve with a dash of garlic powder and a slice of butter for seasoning.

SERVES THREE.

Blue-Collar Salad

1 cup dandelion greens and crowns
½ cup black mustard leaves
½ cup New Zealand spinach
½ cup beets (roots)
½ cup onions, wild or cultivated
Juice of 1 lemon
3 tablespoons olive oil
½ cup shredded swiss cheese
Garlic powder and pepper, to taste

Taste the dandelion and mustard leaves to be certain that they are not yet too bitter to be used raw in salads.

Mix the dandelion leaves and crowns, New Zealand spinach leaves, and the black mustard leaves (torn into bite-size pieces) in a salad bowl. Slice or dice the beets and onions and add them to the bowl. Squeeze the lemon over the salad, add the oil, cheese, and the seasoning and toss. Enjoy it, chew thoroughly, and listen to music to aid your digestion. Then get back to work!

SERVES FOUR.

Sweet Summer Rain

1 cup dandelion leaves and crowns
1 cup lamb's-quarters leaves and tender stems
1 cup dock leaves
1 cup purslane stems and leaves
1 cup watercress
1 onion, sliced
Butter

Collect and rinse all the plants and place in a steamer until done. Add the sliced onion and cook, covered, until tender. Serve with butter.

MAKES FOUR MEDIUM SERVINGS.

Root Coffee

Find a field or lawn full of dandelions. With a digging tool or trowel, loosen the soil around each root. Remove and collect the largest roots and replant the smaller ones. Remove all the adhering soil from the roots. (Dandelion roots are easily washed by placing a canvas bag of them in a briskly flowing river. This won't remove *all* the soil but will save you a lot of work.)

Dry the cleaned roots in the sun, over the campfire coals, or in an oven. When they are thoroughly dry, grind them to a powder. The powder can now be roasted to a deep brown color (like the color of coffee). Percolate your dandelion grounds through a drip coffeemaker.

The grounds can be used by themselves or mixed half and half with coffee grounds. The flavorful, aromatic beverage makes a wonderful campfire brew. Serve with honey, cream, and a cinnamon stick.

DOCK, CURLY DOCK, YELLOW DOCK
(*Rumex crispus*)

Dock is a member of the Buckwheat family (Polygonaceae), which has 48 genera and about 1,200 species worldwide.

The *Rumex* genus has about 190 to 200 species worldwide with 63 occurring in North America.

IDENTIFYING DOCK

Dock is found in agricultural land, swamps, fields, ditches, and vacant lots. It is most easily recognized by the conspicuous chocolate or coffee-brown seed stalk of autumn, which can grow to about 4 feet tall. The seeds are clustered in threes and are attached to papery wings.

The dark green leaves are lanceolate-shaped with a wavy or curly margin. They can measure up to a foot long.

USES

Dock leaves are a bit sour when raw, and they can turn bitter as they mature. The young leaves are good chopped and added to salads. The sour stems provide a tasty trail nibble. The leaves can also be steamed like spinach and served lightly seasoned. When cooking, the leaves turn from green to almost brown. The texture of the cooked leaves is slightly mucilaginous.

Dock leaves go well with onions and tomatoes, in either raw or cooked dishes.

The coffee-colored dock seed stalks are commonly cut and used in dried floral arrangements. I once observed these seed stalks for sale in a floral supply store for about $5 per stalk (adjusted for approximate current value). The dock grew wild in the vacant lots behind and on all sides of this store; possibly the proprietors collected these stalks themselves. An

Young dock leaves, ideal for salads or cooked dishes.

The author next to a patch of ideal dock leaves. PHOTO BY RICK ADAMS.

The young, newly emerging leaves of dock.

observant shopper could certainly save a few dollars by watching vacant lots before laying down dollars on the store counter.

The seeds can be used for flour. They should be collected and winnowed and then ground into a flour. The flour can be used alone, but it is better mixed with another flour such as wheat.

The flower spike of the dock with the seeds still green.

The dock plant with the mature brown seeds.

If you wish to have dock growing in your own yard, simply scatter some of the seeds during the winter, or dig up a wild root and plant it in your yard.

Angeles Forest Lunch

3 cups dock leaves and stems, chopped fine
1 prickly pear cactus pad, peeled and diced
2 cups fresh chickweed, cut into bite-size pieces
1 red onion, diced
2 hard-boiled eggs, sliced thin
2 tomatoes, diced
Light dressing of apple cider vinegar and olive oil
Dash of sea salt and kelp powder

Mix all the ingredients together and then savor this wonderfully flavored and very nutritious salad.

SERVES SIX.

Rim of the World Lunch (Creamed Dock)

1 cup boiled or steamed mustard leaves
2 cups boiled or steamed dock leaves
2 tablespoons butter
2 tablespoons whole-wheat or potato flour
½ onion, diced and cooked
¾ cup milk (can be made from powdered milk)
½ teaspoon salt

Cook the mustard and dock leaves and measure out the correct amount of the cooked leaves. Chop well.

Melt the butter in a skillet (one that has a lid) and add the flour. Mix well, and then add the onion (already cooked and chopped fine), chopped greens, and the milk. Stir and cover for about 5 minutes.

Serve with salt to taste.

SERVES THREE.

Point Reyes Sunset (Dock and Clam Soup)

1 onion, chopped fine
2 cups dock leaves, chopped fine
½ cup watercress, diced
3 cups water
3 cups clams, shucked
2 tablespoons butter
½ cup sea rocket sprouts, gathered from sandy shores (alfalfa sprouts can be substituted)
3 cups milk (powdered milk is okay, cream is ideal)

We made this recipe while camping at Point Reyes National Seashore just north of San Francisco. We collected the dock and watercress along a stream that emptied into the ocean. We purchased the clams from a local merchant who raised them. The real treat in this soup was the sea rocket sprouts. While hiking along the sandy shores of Point Reyes earlier that day, we spotted an old dried sea rocket plant that had gone to seed. Hundreds of the sprouts were growing in the sand under the plant. These were easily collected and washed, and the mild mustard flavor betrayed the plant's relationship to common mustard.

Begin to prepare the soup by dicing the onions, dock, and watercress and adding to the water. Once the water is simmering, add the clams, butter, sprouts, and milk. Then let the soup simmer for about 20 minutes. Don't let it boil.

This is a most delicious soup and many variations of it are possible.

SERVES SIX.

Getting ready to cook tomatoes, onions, and dock leaves.

John Watkins Special (Sweet, Sour, and Salty)

Butter
2 cups coarsely chopped white or red onions
2 cups diced tomatoes
2 cups dock leaves, cleaned and chopped
Garlic powder

Add about 2 tablespoons of butter to your cast-iron or stainless steel skillet. Sauté the onions until they are thoroughly cooked. Don't rush this step—cook them until they actually become "sweet." Keep a lid on the skillet during cooking.

Now add the diced tomatoes, cover, and let cook for about 3 minutes. Add the chopped dock leaves, stir in well, cover, and let cook until the dock leaves have turned from bright green to a brownish green. That will be approximately 5 minutes.

Serving the delicious combination of tomatoes, red onions, and dock leaves.

This simple vegetable mix has a delicious flavor, combining three differently flavored foods that complement each other quite well. This was a favorite of John Watkins, a wild-food forager (among other professions) who grew up in the South.

SERVES THREE.

EPAZOTE (*Dysphania ambrosiodes,* formerly *Chenopodium ambrosiodes*)

Epazote is a member of the Goosefoot family (Chenopodiaceae), which includes 100 genera and 1,500 species worldwide.

The *Dysphania* genus contains about 32 species.

IDENTIFYING EPAZOTE

Once you know the aroma, you can identify epazote in the dark. Look for the multibranched stem about 2 feet tall, and the light green elliptical-shaped leaves (about 2 to 3 inches long) with an undulating and slightly toothed margin. The alternately arranged leaves are sometimes blotched red. If still in doubt, take a leaf to a local college's botany department.

This strongly scented plant is native to the tropics of Mexico and South America, and has now naturalized throughout the southern half of the United States. Hikers will automatically recognize the unique aroma of epazote, for this is the smell associated with streambeds where the plant grows so prolifically.

USES

Epazote is one of the best antiflatulent herbs, yet few Americans are aware of it. Mexicans, especially those living in tropical lowlands, routinely add this herb to their *frijoles* to prevent gas. It is as prized as cilantro. A small sprig of epazote added to beans renders them delicious and "gas-free"; larger quantities of the herb, however, will impart a bitter flavor to the beans.

The growing tips of a young epazote plant.

The leaves of epazote.

A view of the epazote plant growing in a streambed. Note the typical red coloration of the stem.

Epazote growing in a streambed.

Epazote is an annual that is easily cultivated. Collect the wild seeds in late summer or fall by gently stripping the seeds from the mature plant. The seeds are black and tiny, and are formed in dense, spike-like clusters. In the spring, plant the seeds in a moist, well-drained, and partially shaded part of your yard. The plant can also be grown in pots or in a window garden. An ideal location for epazote is under and around a leaky faucet or hose. Just remember that the plant's natural habitat is a streambed, so the cultivated plant will thrive in similar conditions.

To use epazote, collect the fresh, young leaves, preferably well before the plant goes to seed.

Spring is the ideal time, although leaves can be collected throughout the year where it does not snow. To dry, lay the clean leaves on newspaper or brown paper bags, and let dry in a dark place. A closet or an attic, preferably with some ventilation and little humidity, is okay.

Epazote leaves can be added fresh to foods or dried. Into an average pot of beans, crumble about 2 teaspoons of the dried herb or about six fresh leaves.

Epazote can also be made into tea to stop or prevent excessive gas. Infuse 1 teaspoon of the herb in a cup of hot water and drink unsweetened. Epazote tea is effective for expelling intestinal worms (such as roundworms and hookworms) and other intestinal parasites. The herb is said to be less effective against tapeworms.

Farmer Adrian Gaytan grows and sells epazote to his customers at the farmers' markets.

If you have no wild epazote in your area, or if you are unable to identify it, you can investigate seed catalogs under the name epazote, or possibly Jerusalem oak, Mexican tea, wormseed, or Mexican goosefoot.

COOKING WITH EPAZOTE

Cooking with epazote is easy! Add about 1 tablespoon of the herb—both the chopped stems and the leaves—to a pot of beans. You can use it fresh or dried.

The entire epazote plant can be dried and used when the fresh plant is not in season.

The epazote herb can also be added to soups, stews, and made into tea. The powdered leaves can be added to salads, such as potato and bean salads.

Maya Black Bean Soup

1 cup dried black beans
3 onions
3 small potatoes
Pinch of sage
Water
Pinch of oregano
2 teaspoons epazote
Salt and pepper, to taste

Cook the beans first for about an hour until tender. Then add the onions and potatoes, and cook until tender. Add the seasonings. Let simmer on low temperature for 15 minutes before serving.

Lentil Soup

1 cup lentils
1 bay leaf
5–6 cups water
2 teaspoons dried epazote
1 red onion, diced
3 garlic cloves, diced
2 carrots, diced

Wash the lentils, and then simmer with bay leaf in water for an hour and a half. Add the other ingredients when the beans are nearly soft. Simmer until the vegetables are soft. (Add salt or kelp to taste, if desired.)

FENNEL (*Foeniculum vulgare*)

Fennel is a member of the Parsley or Carrot family (Apiaceae, formerly Umbelliferae). This family contains about 300 genera and 3,000 species worldwide. The *Foeniculum* genus contains only one member, fennel.

IDENTIFYING FENNEL

Fennel can grow to a height of 6 feet. Each leaf is finely divided into fern-like leaflets. Each individual segment of the leaf is needle-like, somewhat like a pine needle. The base of each leaf is flared, somewhat like the base of a celery stalk.

The flowers and subsequent seeds are formed in compound umbels, typical of the Parsley family.

USES

Fennel is a tasty, licorice-flavored and -scented plant that resembles dill. It is sometimes called wild anise or wild licorice.

The young, tender shoots of spring are delicious served like celery, possibly with blue cheese dip, peanut butter, or just salt. The tender, succulent lower shoots are most tasty when diced and added to any green salads. These tender shoots can also be diced and mixed into soups and stews.

For a pleasant licorice-flavored tea, add a few seeds of fennel to a mug, pour boiling water into the cup, and by the time the water is cool enough to drink, you'll have a licorice-tasting tea.

When the plant matures and the stalks are too fibrous to eat, you can still peel off an individual leaf and eat the base of the leaf as you'd eat a celery stalk.

I like having fennel in the yard also. Not only does it provide food, but it also imparts a graceful beauty. Fennel can be introduced into your yard by scattering the seeds or by transplanting a root. However, don't

The newly emerging fennel leaves, and last year's dried flower stalks.

Keith Farrar examines a wild fennel plant.

plant in your own yard unless you *really* like it. Fennel can spread quite a bit, and can be very invasive in its growth.

The entire plant has a fern-like appearance, and the overall coloration is light green to almost bluish-green.

The licorice aroma of the entire plant is most characteristic.

Since the Parsley family contains poisonous members (such as hemlock), make absolutely certain that you've positively identified this plant before you take a taste.

Teresa's Savory Dish

1 prickly pear cactus pad
Oil
About 10 pieces of the lower shoot of springtime fennel,
  about 4 to 6 inches in length
½ red onion
Lemon juice to flavor
Garlic powder

In the spring when the fennel plant produces its new growth, collect about 10 new shoots (the lower part below the leaves). These tender and succulent sections are generally about 4 to 6 inches in length and about an inch thick. The ferny leaves are somewhat dry and not as sweet, succulent, and flavorful as the stalks.

Begin by peeling one prickly pear cactus pad. Make certain it is a young, still tender pad. Once the pad is peeled of all its spines and glochids, cut it into small pieces and sauté in some oil. Let it cook on low heat so that some of the water and mucilaginousness of the cactus cooks out. Next, dice the fennel shoots into round segments, in much the way you'd dice green onions. Dice the red onion. Add both the fennel and onion into the skillet with the cactus, and cook until done.

This is a very interesting flavor combination—licorice, sweet onion flavor, and the somewhat green pepper flavor of the cactus. Some people like this with just mild salt or kelp seasoning. Try it with just a squeeze of lemon juice and a dash of garlic powder. This is a very refreshing spring and summertime salad.

SERVES FOUR.

Fennel Crunch

About 2 cups tender fennel shoots
1 garlic clove, diced
1 tablespoon apple cider vinegar
1 tablespoon safflower oil
½ teaspoon dill weed
½ teaspoon paprika
½ teaspoon pepper

Collect the young, tender fennel shoots (not the leaves—just the succulent stalks). Dice them, add the diced garlic, and season with the rest of the ingredients. Mix well.

MAKES EIGHT SMALL SERVINGS.

The umbel of dried fennel seeds. The seeds make a licorice-flavored tea.

Sacramento Vagabond (a Steamed Fennel Dish)

2 potatoes
6 large fennel stalks
6 brussels sprouts
1 large onion
Pepper
Butter

Steam the vegetables until tender. (As an alternative, you can cook in minimal water, then drain the water.) When tender, season with pepper and butter and serve.

SERVES TWO.

FILAREE (*Erodium circutarian, moschatum,* and related species)

Filaree is a member of the Geranium family (Geraniaceae). This family contains six genera and about 750 species worldwide.

The *Erodium* genus contains about 74 species worldwide.

IDENTIFYING FILAREE

Filaree leaves are pinnately divided, and each leaflet is serrated on the margin. The stalks of some species can grow over a foot tall in the spring.

The small flowers are rose to purple colored. The fruits are pin-like and measure about 1 inch long.

USES

Filaree, also called heron's bill or scissors plant, is commonly available in the West. In the East only one species occurs sporadically.

Filaree's tender young leaves and stems are eaten raw in salad. The plant is almost sweet, and it becomes fibrous as it matures. Test some by biting into it; if the stalks are tender, add them to your green salads.

The greens can also be steamed, as you'd steam spinach. Another possibility is to dice the tender stalks and mix them into omelets.

Filaree is a welcome plant found in the springtime throughout the United States. It is most abundant west of the Rockies and is usually found growing in disturbed soils.

The stems are a tasty source of juice and nutrition when chewed along the trail.

The flower of filaree. PHOTO BY RICK ADAMS

Note the linear seed capsules of the maturing filaree plants.

The filaree plant.

An overall view of the filaree plant, often found in dry areas.

Filaree Up (a Health Juice)

1 cup fresh filaree leaves and stems
1 cup fresh lamb's-quarters leaves
1 cup purslane stems and leaves
2 cups carrot juice
1 garlic clove

First, it should be noted that there are two types of juicers. One type (which can be manual or electric) removes all pulp from the juice. That's the type I typically used when I made "Filaree Up." The other type of juicer blends the pulp and juice together, so you need to add water. Keeping the pulp in your juice is actually the healthier choice, so I prefer that method these days.

Collect the fresh wild greens and juice them using whatever method you choose. Then mix this juice with the carrot juice.

If you don't have access to a juicer (or electricity), then chop up the greens and garlic clove very fine. Mix all the greens and carrot juice and garlic together. You may need to reduce the greens or increase the carrot juice to get a juice of desired consistency. This mixture can be lightly simmered over the campfire for a while, and then drunk as a hot tea or even a type of soup.

Again, you need not have electricity in order to make juices. A hand-crank model is available from various manufacturers. You can find one where the Amish do their shopping, at Lehmans.com.

SERVES FOUR.

The young rosette of filaree.

Nathaniel's Filaree Stem Salad

1 cup filaree leaves, including the stems (if still tender)
1 cup purslane stems and leaves
½ cup fennel stalks (the tender lower stalk)
½ cup tender, white inner cattail stalks
1 tomato, diced
½ cup (or so) blue cheese salad dressing

Collect the filaree when the stems are still tender and succulent. Cut the stems and leaves into bite-size pieces and add to your salad bowl. Also dice the purslane stems and leaves, the lower fennel stalks, and the cattail shoots. Add the tomato and mix well. Serve with a topping of blue cheese dressing.

Instead of tomatoes, we've substituted western black nightshade berries (*Solanum douglasii*) that were fully ripe. Also, about a ⅓ cup of watercress stems and leaves makes a spicy addition.

SERVES FOUR.

Filaret

Oil (for the pan)
3 eggs
1½ cup filaree, chopped into bite-size pieces
½ bell pepper, diced
2 garlic cloves, finely diced

Heat an oiled cast-iron skillet. Beat the eggs and pour into the pan. Mix together the chopped filaree, the diced bell pepper, and the finely diced garlic, and place on top of the eggs. Cover the pan and let cook at a low heat. When you can pick up an edge of the omelet, loosen the bottom from the pan. Then fold the omelet in half and let it cook until done. Serve warm with a pickled jalapeño pepper and a rolled, steaming tortilla.

After the pleased diners compliment the chef and offer tips, you can offer a tip of your own: Let everyone know that filaree is not a useless weed to be stomped underfoot, but a fine food in omelets and other dishes.

SERVES TWO.

Self-Reliance (Steamed Greens)

1 cup filaree leaves and stems (if tender)
1 cup tender nettle tops (gather carefully!)
1 cup black mustard leaves
Butter

This is a simple recipe. Rinse all the leaves and tear into large pieces. Steam them all together. When tender, season simply with butter and enjoy.

One man subsisted on variations of these greens and rice for about a 2-week period of unemployment. With great appreciation he savored the "weeds" in his backyard and the rice that he had stored in his pantry. Had he not the simple knowledge of wild food identification, he would have deprived himself of many healthful vitamins and minerals during his period of low funds.

SERVES TWO.

GLASSWORT (*Salicornia* spp.)

Glasswort is a member of the Goosefoot family (Chenopodiaceae), which includes 100 genera and 1,500 species worldwide.

The *Salicornia* genus has approximately 50 species worldwide, mostly found in coastal regions.

IDENTIFYING GLASSWORT

Glasswort is a succulent, leafless plant that appears in coastal areas along both the Pacific and Atlantic coasts. It is also found in the alkaline marshes in the deserts of the Southwest. The slender, greenish stems are jointed with many segments. The plant is branched, and the stems reach up to a foot tall.

The flowers are inconspicuous. In the fall the plants turn red, a sign that the stems are becoming fibrous.

USES

A nibble of a tender glasswort stem reveals a crunchy texture and naturally salted, refreshing flavor. The tender stalks are delicious mixed into most salads, whether they are leafy salads, potato salads, or coleslaw. A few of the tender stalks liven up most sandwiches.

Young glasswort on a beach.

The young, fleshy stems of glasswort.

The plant, when still tender, goes well with cooked foods. It can be simply steamed and served as a vegetable. Or it can be added to soups, omelets, mixed vegetable dishes, and cooked with meats. The tender stalks also make a unique and flavorful pickle.

Note that some of the glasswort stems turn red as the plant matures and produces seed.

As the plant matures, a fibrous core will develop within each stem. When this occurs, you can still pick the stems and chew off the tender outsides of the stems. However, at this stage, you wouldn't want to add these to salads.

Glasswort is often found growing near New Zealand spinach, orach, and even watercress (such as in back bays or where rivers empty into the ocean). All of these plants can be collected and made into a refreshing salad.

Zuma Beach Repast (a Salad)

1 cup glasswort
1 cup New Zealand spinach
½ cup orach (*Atriplex sp.*)
½ cup watercress
½ cup wild or domestic onion, diced
1 ripe tomato, well diced, or ½ cup ripened western black nightshade berries
1 ripe avocado
Dressing of apple cider vinegar and olive oil

Clean and rinse all the wild greens of any sand and then dice them. Add the onions, the tomato or berries, and the avocado, peeled and sliced into thin pieces. Then season with a light dressing. There is no need to add salt to this salad since the first three plants are already "pre-salted."

SERVES FIVE.

Windy Winter Walk (Cooked Greens)

1 cup tender glasswort stems
1 cup New Zealand spinach
½ cup orach leaves (can substitute lamb's-quarters leaves)
½ cup sea rocket sprouts
½ cup sea lettuce seaweed, chopped

Collect all these greens fresh from beach areas and along streams emptying into the ocean. Make certain that the glasswort is still tender.

Put all the leaves into a soup kettle and cook with a little water until tender. Serve with a side of clam chowder or freshly collected and steamed mussels. (Make certain you don't collect mussels in those hotter months when they become toxic.)

Can you feel it? The cold, brisk wind blowing sand in your face . . . the brilliant setting sun reflecting on the water causes you to squint . . . the fresh, salty aroma of the ocean . . . birds singing, swooping, and dancing on the surface of the water. You collected every ingredient for your tasty cooked greens right on the beach. Delicious!

SERVES FOUR.

Glasswort Pickles

2 cups tender glasswort stems
1 quart raw apple cider vinegar
¼ cup honey (raw, unfiltered)
1 sliced onion
1 tablespoon fresh garlic, whole or chopped
1 tablespoon dill weed
Water

To pickle glasswort, first collect the tender young stems. Once cleaned, cut them into bite-size pieces and place them in cleaned jars. The pickling mix is made by combining 1 quart of vinegar, ¼ cup honey, a sliced onion, and pickling spices (garlic, dill, etc.). This mix is boiled for 10 minutes and poured hot over the glasswort until the jars are full.

The full jars are then sealed airtight and kept for at least 2 weeks before serving. If you plan to refrigerate the glasswort pickles, these instructions are adequate. However, if you plan to store the pickles on your pantry shelf, then you'll need to be certain that the whole procedure is done properly. Safe and successful canning requires careful attention to many details, which can be found in a complete cookbook or in a book specifically on home canning of foods.

SERVE AS GARNISH.

LAMB'S-QUARTERS (*Chenopodium album*)

Lamb's-quarters is a member of the Goosefoot family (Chenopodiaceae), which includes 100 genera and 1,500 species worldwide.

The *Chenopodium* genus contains about 100 species worldwide.

IDENTIFYING LAMB'S-QUARTERS

Lamb's-quarters is an annual with an erect stalk. The plant can grow over 5 feet tall, but it usually grows about 3 feet tall.

The plant has a scruffy appearance, and the leaves and stalks are covered with a whitish mealy powder.

Each leaf is roughly triangular in shape, about 2 to 4 inches long. The leaf margin is unevenly toothed, and the leaves are alternately arranged.

The flowers are green and inconspicuous, clustered at the top of the plant in dense spikes. The seeds are small and black.

Occasionally you'll find plants with red coloration along the stems and leaves, and even a completely red plant. The red pigment becomes most prominent in certain situations as a survival mechanism of the plant.

A similar (and similarly edible) lamb's-quarters is green lamb's-quarters (*Chenopodium murale*). Green lamb's-quarters does not grow as tall as common, or white, lamb's-quarters, and its leaves are much glossier green.

Lamb's-quarters belongs to the Goosefoot family, a group of completely nontoxic plants. To varying degrees, they can all be utilized for their edible leaves and seeds.

White lamb's-quarters. Note how rain beads up on the leaves.

White lamb's-quarters in a garden.

Ryan Swank studies the leaf and characteristics of the white lamb's-quarters (*Chenopodium album*).

USES

Lamb's-quarters has pulled through as the main salad ingredient more than any other wild plant we use for meals. This plant is persistent and it will still be growing during drought periods when others have perished. It can survive in sidewalk cracks, dry vacant lots, and disturbed soils across the United States. The plant is a European native, but it has now firmly established North America as home.

The plant is a rich source of vitamins and minerals, and it's a shame that so much is uprooted and tossed into trashcans every spring. Although the plant is somewhat coarser and mealier than farm-cultivated spinach, lamb's-quarters can substitute for spinach in every case.

Add the tender lamb's-quarters leaves and stems to your favorite

A noodle dish with plenty of lamb's-quarters greens.

Lamb's-quarters and other wild greens, sautéed with tomatoes. This makes a great vegetable dish. Eggs can be added if preferred.

To prepare for freezing (for later use), blanch the greens. Clean the leaves, put in a pot, and bring to a boil. Turn off the heat and drain. Pack in freezer bags and freeze. Be sure to date and label the bags.

salad. Roll the hearty leaves into an omelet, or cook it with huevos rancheros. Steamed and served with butter, lamb's-quarters is superb.

Lamb's-quarters makes a good creamed soup. The finely diced leaves can be added to quiche, as pioneered by David Ashley, a fellow self-reliance associate who is aware of the bounty all around us.

In the fall, the seeds of mature lamb's-quarters plants can be easily harvested. Once winnowed, these seeds can be used alone or mixed with other flours for pastry products. Try it in bread and pancakes. [See the Nuts (and Seeds) section for seed recipes.]

It's easy to get a wild patch of lamb's-quarters growing in your yard. In an area of disturbed soil (where you don't often walk), scatter and mix some seeds into the soil. (Although you could scatter seeds anytime, anywhere, the best times would be in the fall before the rains come in the West, and in the spring after the snow melts in the East.) The seeds sprout readily, and most of them will be sprouting in the spring. As you use the plants during the subsequent year, make certain to let at least one plant go to seed, and don't disturb the roots. By taking these simple precautions, you'll be guaranteed a perennial supply of this fine food.

The green lamb's-quarters, *Chenopodium murale*. Also called "nettle-leaf goosefoot."

Sour Lamb

2 quarts lamb's-quarters greens
1 pint sour cream
Garlic powder

Collect lamb's-quarters leaves and tender tops. Steam until tender (about 4 minutes is sufficient), strain, and chop fine. Stir in sour cream, add a dash of garlic powder, and serve warm.

SERVES ABOUT FOUR.

"End of the World" Survival Salad

3 cups lamb's-quarters leaves
½ cup fully ripe western black nightshade berries (or substitute tomatoes, diced)
1 teaspoon mustard seeds, collected from wild plants
½ onion
1 tablespoon apple cider vinegar
1 tablespoon peanut oil

We've made this delicious wild food salad in late fall when there wasn't much else available.

On a particular outing, a *Los Angeles Times* reporter and photographer came along to see the bounty of wild foods right in Los Angeles County. But we saw smoke and heard fire sirens before we all arrived at the outing location. The entire small canyon—exactly where our outing was planned—was in flames. We had chosen the canyon because it was one of the few areas where there was an abundance of green growth in the dry, late summer season.

So we all caravanned up a winding, curving road to another location about 2 miles away, where we felt we'd find enough wild plants to make a meal.

When we arrived at our destination, I quickly scanned the dry chaparral along the trail we'd be walking. We began the outing, and I pointed out the various common chaparral plants, bushes, and shrubs. I was somewhat concerned that the *Los Angeles Times* reporter might be disappointed in our findings, but I let my thinking shift to more important matters. For example, how did the Indians who once roamed these hills sustain themselves in this particular environment? I answered the question before anyone asked: snakes, deer, birds, and lots of acorns from the next canyon over. The participants were getting the feel of what it would actually be like to have to provide one's own meals from the wild. In this particular dusty locale, it was possible, but not easy.

As we hiked along, we tried eating dried mustard leaves. We let them lie on our tongues for a few seconds, and then we chewed the leaves as they became reconstituted. We sampled a few insects. We collected some mustard seeds from the ripe pods on the mature mustard plant.

Fortunately, we found a thick patch of lamb's-quarters, and we carefully picked off the fresh leaves, filling a bag. Farther along, we found a large western black nightshade plant rambling over the sagebrush. We collected a good number of the fully ripened black, tomato-like berries. For our meal, we also collected some white sage leaves and some young prickly pear cactus pads.

We stopped in a shady spot and began to prepare our afternoon wild food meal. Besides a side dish of diced prickly pear cactus pads and the white sage tea, our main dish was lamb's-quarters salad.

We had collected about 3 cups of lamb's-quarters leaves, which we rinsed, diced, and put into the salad bowl. We added the ripe western black nightshade berries, and about 1 teaspoon of freshly harvested mustard seeds. We had carried an onion along in our pack, so we diced up half of it and put it in the salad. We seasoned the salad with a little oil and vinegar from our pack, and then we mixed the salad ingredients.

It was a delicious salad that we all shared. The reporter got her story, and the rest of us gained a deep feeling of appreciation for the plants that provided us sustenance in this seemingly desolate environment.

MAKES SIX MEDIUM SERVINGS.

Sunday Brunch

4 cups lamb's-quarters greens, chopped
4 tablespoons grated cheddar cheese
2 tablespoons apple cider vinegar
1 teaspoon kelp powder

Steam the lamb's-quarters greens. (Tender stems can also be used.) Mix in the cheese and vinegar and let cook in a closed container until the cheese melts. Sprinkle the kelp powder over the greens before serving.

Serve alongside small watercress sandwiches for Sunday brunch.

MAKES ABOUT FIVE SMALL SERVINGS.

Julie Balaa looks at two similar-looking wild plants growing side-by-side: On the left, the black nightshade (*Solanum spp.*), which can cause sickness if not properly cooked, and on the right, green lamb's-quarters, *Chenopodium murale*.

Gould Mesa Deluxe

Butter, as needed
1 onion, diced
¼ cup apple cider vinegar
¼ teaspoon pepper
¼ teaspoon paprika
¼ teaspoon powdered kelp
3 cups lamb's-quarters leaves and tender stems

Melt the butter in a cast-iron skillet. Add the diced onion and vinegar, and cook until the onion is tender. Add the seasoning and the lamb's-quarters leaves, and cook until the greens are tender.

SERVES THREE.

Campfire Repast

Oil (for the pan)
3 cups lamb's-quarters leaves and tender stems
1 onion, cut into round slices
Chia seeds
Lemon juice or butter

Warm a cast-iron skillet over the fire and oil the pan. (If you don't have oil, just put a little bit of water in the bottom of the pan.) Put the lamb's-quarters leaves into the pan after you've torn them into large pieces. Lay the onion slices on top and cover the skillet. When the onions are tender, it's ready to serve. Sprinkle a few chia seeds over each plate of the cooked lamb's-quarters and onion, and season lightly with lemon juice or butter.

This makes an excellent addition to freshly caught and baked fish.

SERVES TWO.

Alpine Glow (a Salad)

2 cups lamb's-quarters leaves and tender stems
1 cup purslane stems and leaves
1 prickly pear cactus pad, still young and tender
½ onion, diced
2 tablespoons salad oil
2 tablespoons apple cider vinegar
Garlic powder

We've made many variations of this simple salad recipe in summer and early fall when many of the spring greens were no longer available. Simply clean and chop the leaves and mix them together. Peel the prickly pear pad and dice it into small pieces. (Be careful not to get the spines or glochids into your skin.) Add the diced onion, the oil and vinegar, and the garlic powder. Mix all the ingredients well. Serve with a baked potato and watercress soup.

White sage or ginseng tea would be a good addition to this meal.

SERVES THREE OR FOUR.

MALLOW (*Malva* spp.)

Mallow is a member of the Mallow family (Malvaceae). This family contains 266 genera and 4,025 species worldwide.

The *Malva* genus contains about 30 to 40 species worldwide. Probably the most notable are *Malva neglecta* (common mallow) and *Malva parviflora* (cheeseweed).

IDENTIFYING MALLOW

Malva can be found throughout the United States in fields, barnyards, vacant lots, roadsides, disturbed soils, gardens, and occasionally in sidewalk cracks.

The plant is highly branched, sometimes forming green mounds that rise to about 3 feet.

The leaves are roundish in outline, and palmately divided into 7 to 11 shallow lobes. The leaf margin is finely toothed. Each leaf stalk is quite long—commonly three or four times as long as the leaf blade.

The pale lilac or rose-colored flowers are five-petaled. They are arranged in close axillary clusters along the stalk.

The fruits are most characteristic, resembling round packages of cheese since the round fruits, when mature, readily break up into triangular cheese-like segments.

The round leaves of mallow and the young seeds.

A close-up of the round "cheeses" of mallow seeds.

Julie Balaa examines the flowers of the wild mallow.

USES
There are approximately 30 to 40 different species of mallow, and all can be similarly used. However, I typically use *Malva neglecta*, the common mallow of the urban setting.

The leaves can be chewed raw for coughs or minor sore throats. The slightly sticky texture of the plant helps to soothe the throat.

The leaves are edible raw in salads, and they can be prepared in most ways: steamed, cooked in soup, added to omelets, and even chopped fine and added to quiche.

One mallow variety is common in the deserts, making a welcome addition to the often sparse desert salad bowl.

Small fruits develop on the mallow that resemble tiny packets of cheese. These fruits are edible raw as nibblers or they can be added to salad. The flavor is somewhat bland, but the texture does bear a slight resemblance to cheese.

Mallow, also called cheeseweed or malva, has an interesting relative—marsh mallow (*Althea officinalis*). Marsh mallows are inhabitants of Atlantic coast salt marshes and rivers. At one time, the boiled extract from the root of this plant was whipped up into an egg-white-like froth. This was used for treating sore throats, coughing, and even bronchitis; this original "marshmallow" was a medicine, not the junk-food candy it is today.

A view of the overall mallow plant.

Satisfying Mallow (a Soup)

2 cups water
1 onion bulb (or a bunch of wild onion greens)
2 small Jerusalem artichokes
2 cups mallow leaves, finely chopped
2 cups milk (or cream)
1 bay leaf
Powdered kelp

Heat the water in a saucepan. Dice the onion, cut the Jerusalem artichokes into small pieces, and add both to the pan. Cook at a low heat until the Jerusalem artichoke is almost completely tender. Add the mallow leaves, the milk (or cream), and the bay leaf and kelp for seasoning.

You can use powdered milk to make the milk for this recipe if you are out on the trail or holed up in your cellar until the fallout danger recedes.

MAKES FOUR MEDIUM SERVINGS.

Chaparral Salad

3 cups mallow leaves, stems removed
1 prickly pear cactus pad
2 fresh tomatoes, diced
½ red onion, diced
2 tablespoons olive oil
1 teaspoon apple cider vinegar
Dash of pepper
Powdered seaweed to taste

Collect the mallow leaves, rinse them, and tear into bite-size pieces. Peel one young prickly pear cactus pad (make certain you've removed all the spines and glochids) and then dice it into small pieces. Add the tomatoes and onion. Mix in the oil and vinegar, and then add a dash of pepper (ideally, freshly ground) and seaweed to taste.

We've made variations of this salad many times on Wild Food Outings. Carrying along onion and dressing ingredients in our pack, we'd find mallow and prickly pear and collect enough for everyone on the outing. Instead of tomatoes, we'd use the fresh fruits of the western black nightshade (*Solanum douglasii*), making certain that they were all completely ripe.

Incidentally, this is a good salad to eat if you have a sore throat; both the mallow and the prickly pear, which are somewhat sticky, help to soothe sore throats and coughs.

SERVES THREE.

The author examines an unusually tall mallow plant. PHOTO BY FRANCISCO LOAIZA.

Mallow and Potatoes

2 large potatoes
5 cups mallow leaves, torn into bite-size pieces
½ pint of sour cream
Dill weed

Boil the potatoes until tender, and steam the mallow greens until tender (2 or 3 minutes is sufficient for mallow greens). You can cook both of these together if you need to, adding the mallow when the potatoes are almost done. Drain the water from the potatoes and mallow and place into a serving dish. Mix in the sour cream and top with a sprinkle of dill weed.

Serve immediately, while it's still warm.

SERVES THREE.

Fruity Mallow

2 cups mallow leaves, finely diced
¼ cup mallow "cheeses" or fruits
2 ripe prickly pear fruits, peeled of the outer skin and spines, diced
1 bunch grapes
2 bananas, diced into round slices
2 tablespoons honey
½ cup cream
Sprinkle of cinnamon

Mallow can be used in this delicious fruit salad. Combine all the ingredients except the cinnamon in a salad bowl, including the honey and cream, and toss gently before serving. Or you can add the honey and cream to each individual serving, topping with a sprinkle of cinnamon.

SERVES FOUR.

MILKWEED, COMMON (*Asclepias syriaca, Asclepias californica*)

Milkweed was formerly classified as a member of the Milkweed family, but is now classified as a member of the Dogbane family (Apocynaceae). This family contains 200 to 450 genera and 3,000 to 5,000 species worldwide.

The *Asclepias* genus contains about 100 species worldwide.

IDENTIFYING MILKWEED

Milkweed usually grows erect, from 2 to 5 feet tall. Its overall color is whitish-green, and the leaves are covered with a soft tomentose hair. Each leaf is egg-shaped (ovate to oblong), opposite or whorled, and untoothed at the margins.

Thick milky sap oozes out from the leaves and stems when cut or broken.

USES

Common milkweed is a perennial herb, found most abundantly in the eastern United States. Other species can also be found throughout the United States. The leaf surfaces are softly covered with fine hairs, and the plant is readily identified when you cut the leaf or stem and observe the thick white sap drip out.

The milkweed is best eaten when young. However, it cannot be used in salads because the raw plant is usually too bitter for most people. The best

Milkweed with flower buds.

way to remove the bitterness is to drop the leaves, tender shoots, buds, and pods into boiling water. Let cook for about 2 or 3 minutes, and then drain the water. This process should be repeated at least twice; check to see if the milkweed is then palatable for you.

Once the bitterness is removed, the cooked plant can be added to stews and soups or simply served with butter. The young buds and tender pods make good vegetables by themselves.

A milkweed plant growing in a field.

A patch of milkweed.

There seems to be some controversy over the relative bitterness of this plant. I personally don't care for it raw—but if you enjoy the raw flavor, you should experiment with it raw, and with less boiling.

Cattle have been poisoned by grazing on the raw milkweed, but animals generally avoid this plant. Although there is some debate about the toxicity of *raw* milkweed for humans, I suggest that you err on the side of caution: Never eat milkweed raw, to avoid stomach and intestinal upsets.

The white-, pink-, or rose-colored flowers are arranged in round clusters called umbels. Each flower is five-petaled.

The mature milkweed pods, with the mature seeds now spreading. Pods are no longer edible at this stage, but the downy material attached to the seed can be used for insulation and fire-starting.

A rough-skinned fruits measure about 3 inches long. They can be cooked and eaten while still firm; when the seeds are developed inside, the fruits are inedible.

Camping on the River

2 cups milkweed leaves and tender shoots
½ cup milkweed flower clusters, still tight
1 cup dock leaves
1 cup watercress leaves
½ onion
Butter

Since the milkweed is bitter, the first step is to drop the milkweed leaves, shoots, and flowers into boiling water. Cook for 3 minutes, drain the water, and pour boiling water into the pot over the milkweed. Bring to a boil and let cook for another 3 minutes. This should reduce the bitterness significantly.

After this approximate 6 minutes of cooking, add the other leaves and the onion, all diced into bite-size pieces.

When everything is tender, drain the water, and serve with a bit of butter.

SERVES THREE.

Atop the Indian Mound

1 dozen young, hard milkweed pods
1 carrot, grated
1 tablespoon butter
Pepper

Collect the young milkweed pods that have not begun to mature and go to seed. (Cut one open to be certain.) The pods are bitter and will need to be cooked. To do this properly so the bitterness is removed, you'll need to first bring a pot of water to a boil. Drop in the pods and let cook for only about 2 minutes. Drain the water, remove the pods, and bring fresh water to a boil again. Return the pods to the water, let boil for about 2 minutes, and again, drain the water and remove the pods. If still bitter, repeat the process.

Now add the grated carrots and let cook until the carrots are just slightly cooked. (If you have a steamer, use it for this last step. Otherwise, just cook it all in your pot with a small amount of water.) Season the milkweed pods with the butter and a shake of pepper.

This may seem like a lot of trouble, but milkweed pods do have their own unique flavor that many people enjoy. Also, the pods are a fairly abundant food (in some parts of the country) during the summer. Try them and see for yourself.

During my time living on my grandfather's Ohio farm, I would pick these young pods, cook them, and eat them while sitting atop the prominent Indian mound just west of the fruit orchard.

SERVES TWO.

The young leaves and immature flower buds of the milkweed can be cooked and eaten.

A Tribute to Asclepius

2 large knotty potatoes
1 cup wild garlic or wild onion bulbs
1 Jerusalem artichoke
2 cups young, unopened milkweed flower buds
½ cup milkweed leaves
½ cup New Zealand spinach
Pepper to taste
Butter

Gently boil the potatoes, onions, and Jerusalem artichoke in minimal water. When tender, add the unopened flower buds and leaves of milkweed. (All parts of the milkweed must be processed with hot water, as described in the preceding recipe, to remove the bitterness before being added to the pot.) Add the leaves of New Zealand spinach, and let all the ingredients simmer until tender.

Serve with a dash of pepper and a pat of butter.

Socrates' last request was that his friend, Crito, pay a tribute to Asclepius, the god who heals. Milkweed's genus name is the same as this Greek god of medicine, so it is only proper to ponder deeply that which heals as we partake of this meal.

This dish is best eaten in the open, sitting on a rock, with the sun bright, the wind light, and your thoughts aflight.

SERVES FOUR.

Early Summer Stew

Butter, as needed
1 cup wild onion greens and bulbs (or 1 garden onion)
2 cups firm milkweed pods, processed to remove bitterness
2 tomatoes, diced
1 cup purslane stems and leaves, diced
1 cup tender mustard leaves
Kelp powder
Marjoram (preferably fresh)

Dice the onion. Slice the preprocessed milkweed pods. Warm your skillet and lightly butter it. Add the onions and milkweed pods and gently sauté. In about 5 minutes, add the tomatoes and purslane and continue to sauté. When all is just about done, add the mustard leaves, torn into bite-size pieces. Cook until the mustard greens are well wilted. Serve seasoned with a dash of kelp and a small amount of fresh marjoram sprinkled over the top.

SERVES THREE.

Cheese Pods

2 cups young milkweed pods
½ cup purslane stems
½ cup wild onions (bulbs and leaves)
½ cup jack or cheddar cheese, grated
Dash of pepper
Dash of paprika
Dash of dill

First process the pods by dropping them into boiling water, cooking for about 3 minutes, and repeating this until the pods are not bitter. Usually, the pods are palatable with two or three boilings. Be sure to select only the young, firm pods; older pods have begun to mature and they are inedible.

Place the processed pods, purslane stems, and onions in a steamer and steam until all are tender. If you don't have a steamer, you can cook them in a covered pot in a small amount of water.

Mix in the cheese and seasonings while the dish is still hot so the cheese begins to melt.

Serve immediately.

SERVES ABOUT THREE.

MINER'S LETTUCE (*Claytonia perfoliata,* formerly *Montia perfoliata*)

Miner's lettuce was formerly classified in the Purslane family, but is now classified as part of the Miner's Lettuce family (Montiaceae). The Miner's Lettuce family contains about 22 genera and about 230 species.

The *Claytonia* genus contains 27 species.

IDENTIFYING MINER'S LETTUCE

Miner's lettuce is an annual that normally reaches a height of about 12 inches. The unmistakable characteristic is the cup or saucer-shaped leaf on the flowering stalk. The flower stalk grows right through this circular leaf. The younger leaves are either triangular or quadrangular. The leaf stalks are from 3 to 12 inches long.

The small white to pink flowers measure about ¼ inch across, growing together in tight clusters along the stalk in racemes. There are five petals per flower.

The upper part of the root and the lower leaves are often a translucent pink color.

USES

Miner's lettuce is a beautiful plant that cannot be mistaken for anything else—the cup-shaped leaves on the flowering stalk are most characteristic. The plant is found from Alaska to Mexico, from the Rocky Mountains to the Pacific Ocean. Miners during the gold rush days used this plant for salad and cooked greens. The plant is most palatable raw, and it can be cooked or steamed as you'd use

Miner's lettuce. PHOTO BY RICK ADAMS.

A huge miner's lettuce leaf. The round leaf of miner's lettuce, with the flower stalk coming through the middle, makes this an easy-to-recognize plant. PHOTO BY GARY GONZALES.

Each miner's lettuce plant consists of many succulent stems that arise from the root, perhaps giving rise to the notion that each plant is like a "head" of lettuce.

any other green. The fresh and cooked miner's lettuce plant not only balanced out the meals of these '49ers, but it also served as their source for much-needed vitamins and minerals, especially vitamin C.

The entire above-ground plant is used. The stems, flowering stalks, and leaves are edible. The flavor and texture are mild, maybe a bit tart, and enjoyed by all.

The plant makes a delicious salad by itself with a light oil and vinegar dressing. Lightly steamed, the plant rivals spinach. Miner's lettuce does not become fibrous or bitter with age; rather, it simply begins to decay. Use only the fresh, sound leaves.

Being so pleasantly flavored and textured, miner's lettuce can be sautéed with other vegetables, mixed into omelets, added to meat and potato stews, and used raw, like lettuce, wherever you use lettuce.

I've had some success in growing miner's lettuce in an urban backyard. I collected some seeds from the mountains of Southern California and planted them in a partially shaded, well-drained area of my yard. Sure enough, several miner's lettuce plants came up in the spring. I ate some of those leaves, but I left the rest to go to seed. This plant can be successfully grown in western states. I planted mine in a relatively small plot that was heavily mulched with leaves.

Once, while conducting a Wild Food Outing in a vacant lot in downtown Pasadena, California, I observed a fairly big patch of large and lush miner's lettuce. It really surprised me to see the plant in an urban setting. It was growing

Young miner's lettuce.

under trees, and the soil seemed quite moist. I returned to that vacant lot several times over the following years, and the miner's lettuce had successfully reseeded itself. But alas, "progress"! That once strong and rich patch of urban miner's lettuce is now buried beneath a freeway off-ramp.

Miner's Delight

3 cups fresh miner's lettuce—the entire above-ground plant
2 hard-boiled eggs, sliced
1 tablespoon mayonnaise
1 tablespoon olive oil (or other quality oil)
Sprinkle of dill weed

Collect the miner's lettuce and rinse it of any adhering sand or soil. Use all of the plant above the ground. Chop the plant, or tear it into bite-size bits. Add the sliced hard-boiled eggs. Toss with mayonnaise and oil, and then sprinkle dill weed over the top.

Miner's lettuce makes a tasty, satisfying salad. The addition of eggs and oil makes this dish all the more nutritious.

SERVES THREE.

Richard's Salad

4 cups fresh miner's lettuce—the entire above-ground plant
½ onion

DRESSING

2 tablespoons oil
2 tablespoons wine vinegar
1 teaspoon powdered dill
½ teaspoon paprika
¼ teaspoon salt
¼ teaspoon pepper
1 teaspoon parsley flakes

Collect the fresh miner's lettuce carefully, and rinse the plants of all sand. Dice the plant into bite-size pieces and put into your salad bowl. Dice up the onion (or use approximately ⅓ cup wild onion leaves and bulbs) and add to salad bowl.

All the dressing ingredients can be mixed together and kept in a small container about the size of a spice jar. If you plan to carry this in your pack (when backpacking), make sure you use an unbreakable container.

Pour the dressing over the salad, mix well, and enjoy an excellent lunch. Small diced pieces of cheese can also be added.

My brother Richard often enjoyed this salad on his spring hikes into the foothills of the Angeles National Forest. He would premix the dressing, carry along the onion, and find the greens in spring. This salad is perfect by itself but can be served with a sandwich or a bowl of soup.

ONE SERVING, IF RICHARD IS PRESENT. OTHERWISE, SIX SERVINGS.

Miner's Spinach

3 cups fresh miner's lettuce—the entire above-ground plant
½ teaspoon pepper
½ teaspoon garlic powder
Butter

Miner's lettuce makes a truly delectable cooked green. The flavor is subtle, the texture is pleasant, and no one will refuse it. Simply steam the greens and season mildly with pepper, garlic powder, and butter.

If you live in an area where you have ready access to the plant each spring, miner's lettuce will become a regular staple in your diet.

SERVES TWO.

Miners in Search of Gold

2 large gold potatoes, quartered
1 cup wild onions, leaves and bulbs, fibrous parts removed
4 cups freshly gathered miner's lettuce—the entire above-ground plant
3 eggs, hard-boiled

Here's a good and satisfying dinnertime vegetable dish to savor after a day of mining or panning gold. Boil the potatoes in a little water. When the potatoes are almost done, add the onions and the miner's lettuce, chopped into bite-size pieces. While the onions and miner's lettuce are simmering, boil the eggs.

When all is done, scoop some of the potato, onion, and miner's lettuce mix onto each plate (with a little of the liquid in the pot). Peel and slice the eggs and serve alongside the cooked vegetables.

This is good with a side of beans and a steamed tortilla.

SERVES THREE.

MUSTARD (*Brassica* spp.)

Mustard is a member of the Mustard family (Brassicaceae). The Mustard family is another large family, comprising more than 330 genera worldwide and about 3,780 species.

The *Brassica* genus contains 35 species.

IDENTIFYING MUSTARD

When in flower, the (usually) yellow flowers make this a most conspicuous spring plant. Upon close inspection, you'll see that the flowers are composed of four sepals, four colorful petals, six stamens (four are tall, and two are short), and one pistil. This is the typical floral pattern of the entire Mustard family.

The leaves are typically lyrately pinnate—that is, there is a large, rounded end lobe on each leaf and smaller lateral lobes. The upper leaves are commonly entire, meaning without lobes or indentations.

Mustards grow from 2 feet up to 6 feet in ideal conditions.

The young mustard plant. Note the shape of the leaves.

USES

True mustards, members of the *Brassica* genus, are annuals native to Europe, North Africa, and Asia. They are now fully naturalized throughout North America.

Both the flavor and texture of the various species of mustard are highly variable. Generally, all mustards have a pungent flavor reminiscent of common radishes. But

Closer view of the shape of mustard leaves.

this radish flavor can range from hot enough to open your sinuses and make your eyes water to pleasantly mild flavored and suitable in salads. The textures can range from very tender to coarse, rough, and hairy.

A species of *Brassica* with exceptionally large leaves, in part due to a wet winter. PHOTO BY HELEN W. NYERGES.

The mustard leaves are suitable in salads when they are young and tender. However, even older leaves can be used in salads if used sparingly and chopped fine.

Cooked mustard greens are well known and enjoyed by generations of Southerners and residents of Appalachia. The leaves are most easily prepared by simply steaming or by sautéing in a skillet with a bit of bacon fat or ham.

The leaves can be minced and used in soups, just as you'd use watercress. The more tender leaves are also good in omelets and even sandwiches.

Mustard flowers. The tender flowers can be picked off and added to soups, salads, and other dishes.

Tips of the still-tender mustard plants are great in soups, sautéed, and in egg dishes.

The dried mustard pods.

Mustard flowers and the unopened buds (which resemble broccoli, but smaller) add color and flavor to salads.

The seeds can be collected from the mature pods, winnowed, and added to salads or cooked foods. Or they can be ground to a powder and mixed with vinegar, water, and other spices to make your own mustard condiment. The tender stalks are also edible, either raw or cooked.

These are mustard seeds that have been extracted from the dried mustard pods, after several winnowings. Seeds can be ground and used as a spice, or simply added to other dishes.

Mustard is a versatile plant that is worth getting to know. It is easily recognized, and it is widely distributed throughout the world.

I can recall one Wild Food Outing when mustard was the only plant we could find to cook. We collected a pot of leaves, began the fire, and started cooking our meal. The leaves were old and somewhat fibrous, but we mixed in some onion slices. Even cooked, these leaves were very spicy and still a bit tough. In spite of a few grumblings, most of us consumed our starlight vegetable dish in appreciation of this one hardy plant called mustard. (The alternative was hunger.)

Mustard Memories

2 quarts mustard leaves
½ onion, in slices
Salt and pepper to taste

Collect the younger lower leaves of mustard and rinse them. Add the leaves and the onion slices to a pot; steam or boil until tender. Season with salt and pepper to taste. A slice of butter or a spoonful of mayonnaise can also be added.

SERVES THREE.

Mustard and Sour Cream Dip

½ cup raw mustard leaves and flower buds, pureed in a blender or finely diced
2 pints sour cream
1 teaspoon garlic powder
Dash of salt

Mix all the ingredients together and use as a dip for potato chips, french fries, tortilla chips, or crackers. It also makes a good spread on toast, and by adding sliced cucumbers it makes a good sandwich spread.

French Mustard Salad

3 cups black mustard leaves
1 cup black mustard's yellow flowers
1 cup mallow leaves
½ cup sow thistle leaves
French dressing

I was both surprised and impressed with how delicious this salad was. Fellow forager Drew Devereux was taking a group of his students into the foothills of the San Gabriel Mountains of Los Angeles County. We saw and discussed a great many plants, but not that many were available at that time of the year for salad. We collected the tender black mustard leaves and the tender yellow flowers. We later found some still-young sow thistle and tested it for bitterness. Since it was still tasty raw, we collected some of the leaves. Mallow leaves were also collected.

When we got back to our campsite, we rinsed all the leaves and tore them into bite-size pieces. With a smile, Drew produced a bottle of french salad dressing from his daypack, and he poured some into our salad bowl. We gently tossed the simple salad, and everyone declared it delicious indeed!

WE SERVED SIX WITH THE ABOVE PROPORTIONS, BUT THEY WERE SMALL SERVINGS.

Burwood Hill

Butter, as needed
3 large red or golden potatoes
2 large onions
2 cups mustard greens

Warm a cast-iron skillet and butter it lightly. Thinly slice the potatoes and lay them in the pan. Thinly slice the onions and lay them over the potatoes. Cover and allow to cook slowly until almost completely tender. Then rinse the mustard greens, tear them into bite-size pieces, and add them to the skillet. Cover again and cook until all is done.

The dish can be covered with a handful of shredded cheese before serving.

We've served this with chicken, and once as a side dish with spaghetti.

Note: Besides common mustard greens (*Brassica* spp.), any member of the Mustard family whose leaves are young and tender can be used in place of mustard.

SERVES ABOUT FOUR.

NASTURTIUM (*Tropaeolum majus*)

Nasturtium is a member of the Tropaeolum family (Tropaeolaceae), which contains only this genus, with about 90 species worldwide.

IDENTIFYING NASTURTIUM

Nasturtium is an ivy-like plant, sprawling over a hillside, climbing over trellises and fences, and adding color to a garden border. The conspicuous flowers are red, orange, and yellow. There are five petals per flower.

The leaves are round-shaped. They are typically 2 to 3 inches in diameter, but in wet years, they can be up to 5 inches in diameter. The light green succulent leaves are alternately arranged on the stalk. The long and succulent leaf stalks are attached to the undersides of the leaves, usually slightly off-center.

USES

Nasturtium is a Peruvian native that has now naturalized in some coastal areas and is commonly grown in ornamental gardens. It grows sprawling and vine-like, seldom over 5 or 6 inches tall.

All parts of the succulent above-ground plant can be eaten. The plant is best used in salads for it imparts a refreshing hotness. Add the leaves, stems, flowers, and fruits to salads.

The leaves, stems, and flowers can be added to egg dishes, cooked vegetable dishes, and soups.

The beautiful nasturtium flowers.

Either raw or cooked, the plant is hotter than expected, so use it sparingly at first.

Nasturtium Cheese Spread

1 bunch small radishes
1 tablespoon nasturtium leaves, finely chopped
1 teaspoon lemon juice
8 ounces cream cheese
Bread or crackers

Wash one bunch of radishes and then coarsely grate them, leaving a few for garnish. Quickly blend with the radishes the nasturtium leaves, lemon juice, and cream cheese.

A view of the nasturtium plant in a garden.

This spread should be used as quickly as possible after being made, since the radishes tend to lose their texture and the nasturtium leaves tend to become slightly bitter. If used promptly, this is a most delectable spread.

Spread over rye or pumpernickel bread, or onto Ry-Krisp, Ak-Mak, or other "natural" crackers.

MAKES ABOUT 1 CUP OF SPREAD.

Nasturtium Zinger Spread

1 cup nasturtium leaves, stems, and flowers, chopped fine
1 cup onions, chopped fine
½ cup common store-bought mushrooms (*Agaricus bisporus*), chopped fine
Several tablespoons of either top-quality mayonnaise or cream cheese

Mix the nasturtium, onions, and mushrooms well with either mayonnaise or cream cheese and spread it on toast.

A slight variation is to use sour cream instead of mayonnaise or cream cheese. Add enough sour cream to make a fairly light consistency. Add a teaspoon of garlic powder and the mashed pulp of one avocado. This can be used as a dip for crackers, potato chips, french fried potatoes, or even as a salad dressing.

SERVES ABOUT EIGHT.

The three-part nasturtium seed somewhat resembles a brain! The tender seeds can be added as a garnish to soups and salads, or pickled and served as a "caper." Or, you can just let them drop and most will sprout up the next season.

Spring Equinox Salad

6 potatoes
2 onions
3 hard-boiled eggs
1 pickle
1 cup nasturtium stems, leaves, and flowers

DRESSING

2 tablespoons safflower oil
2 tablespoons apple cider vinegar
½ teaspoon pepper
2 garlic cloves, finely diced
3 tablespoons mayonnaise
1 tablespoon mustard (try to buy it without yellow dye or make it yourself)
Paprika

Essentially, this is a typical potato salad recipe with fresh nasturtium leaves added. You can mix nasturtium leaves into any potato salad recipe with good results.

Boil the potatoes and onions and cut into small pieces in your salad bowl. Dice up two of the hard-boiled eggs into the salad bowl and save one for a topping. Dice one pickle into small cubes and add to the other ingredients. Chop the nasturtium into very fine pieces and add to the salad.

For the dressing, combine the oil, vinegar, pepper, garlic cloves, mayonnaise, and mustard. Mix into the salad and then lay the slices of one hard-boiled egg on top. Serve warm or chilled.

This is not a recipe you'd make when you're camping or backpacking (although if you were car-camping, you could very likely have all the ingredients in your portable cooler). For a simpler potato salad recipe, see Trail Potato Salad on the next page.

SERVES ABOUT EIGHT.

Wake-Up Salad

1 cup nasturtium leaves, stems, and flowers
1 cup chickweed
½ cup wild radish leaves
½ cup sweet alyssum flowers
½ onion, diced
6 radishes, quartered
2 tablespoons oil
2 tablespoons apple cider vinegar
1 teaspoon garlic powder
1 teaspoon fresh basil, chopped
½ teaspoon pepper

Rinse all the greens and tear into bite-size pieces; put in a salad bowl. Add the sweet alyssum flowers, then add the onion and the radishes. Add the seasoning ingredients and mix well. You can also add garden lettuce to this tasty salad.

SERVES FIVE.

Trail Potato Salad

3 large golden potatoes
¾ cup nasturtium leaves and stems
Approximately ½ cup cheddar cheese, shredded
Garlic powder to taste
Pepper to taste

Boil the potatoes in a covered pot. When nearly done, drain most of the water, leaving just a little water in the bottom of the pot. Cut the potatoes into smaller cubes and return them to the pot. Finely chop the nasturtium stems and leaves and mix them in. Cover the pot and let it simmer for about 5 minutes, or until the nasturtium is wilted.

Add the shredded cheese, garlic powder, and pepper and gently mix it all together. Remove the pot from the heat, keeping the pot covered.

Serve after 5 minutes, when cheese is soft and melting.

SERVES TWO.

NETTLE (*Urtica dioica*)

Nettle is a member of the Nettle family (Urticaceae). This family consists of 50 genera and 700 species worldwide.

Urtica consists of about 45 species worldwide.

IDENTIFYING NETTLE

The usually unbranched stalks of nettle can reach up to 5 feet tall when mature.

The leaves are oblong in shape, tapered to a point, and sharp-toothed on the margins. The leaf surface is covered with hair-like needles. The leaves are arranged opposite each other.

The inconspicuous tiny green flowers are formed in clusters in the axils.

Nettles are perennial plants that grow all over the United States, commonly near water.

USES

Be careful when you collect nettles! When you brush against the plant, the tips of the numerous hair-like needles break off, releasing formic acid onto your skin. This causes an immediate rash sensation, lasting approximately an hour. Wear gloves or use some protection when collecting this plant.

Nettles are not used in salads; they are used as cooked vegetables. Collect the tender tops and steam until cooked. These are delicious when served with butter, and the plant is unable to cause a rash when cooked.

A young nettle plant.

Note the sharp-toothed leaf margins.

A patch of tender nettles.

Farmer Adrian Gaytan sells bundles of nettles at his farmers' market booth. His urban customers are discovering the many virtues of this nutritious plant.

Student Ryan Swank examines the hollow follicles of the nettle plant, which release formic acid when you brush up against them.

The author collects and uses nettles when in season. For off-season use, he dries the plant, and then uses the leaves both in soup and in tea.

Monticello Sunrise (a Soup)

2 cups tender nettle tops
2 tablespoons butter
Milk, approximately ¼ cup (can use powdered milk)
½ cup potato, soy, or whole-wheat flour
1 bay leaf (ideally, gathered fresh)

Rinse and steam the nettle tops. When cooked, cut into very small pieces. Melt the butter in your pan and add a little bit of milk. Slowly add the flour, stirring so no lumps form. Add the nettles and then add enough milk to reach a desired consistency. Add one bay leaf and then let the soup simmer for about 15 minutes. Do not let it boil.

SERVES TWO.

Tender nettle tops have been washed, and will be diced and then added to a soup. A simple nettle soup consists of a miso base, with some small potatoes added.

Nettled Spinach

4 cups tender young nettle tops
Water
Garlic powder
Butter

Carefully collect the youngest, most tender tops of the nettle plant. Use gloves or a brown paper bag for collecting.

Steam or boil the nettles until tender. Drain, lightly season with garlic powder, and serve with butter. These are most delicious if the plant is still tender when collected.

SERVES TWO OR THREE.

Millard Creek Memories (Creamed Nettles)

1 cup nettle greens
1 can cream of mushroom soup (can be made from a dry soup mix)
¼ cup parsley, chopped fine
1 garlic clove, finely diced

Cook the nettles and chop them up fine. Measure 1 cup of the chopped greens and put in your soup pot with the can of soup. You can add water if you like a thinner stock. If you don't have cream of mushroom soup, you can use milk or even powdered milk instead.

No milk? Then use water—you'll just have a thinner stock. Add the parsley and garlic clove. Let simmer but do not boil. This is excellent served with toast.

SERVES TWO.

Altadena Meadows Casserole.

Altadena Meadows Casserole

3 potatoes
2 eggs
1½ cups young, tender nettles
¼ cup grated Parmesan cheese

Steam, bake, or boil the potatoes. Hard-boil the eggs. Lightly steam the nettles until they are tender.

Cut the potatoes and nettles into bite-size pieces and slice the eggs. Into a baking dish, add the potatoes, eggs, and nettles. Sprinkle it all with cheese, cover, and bake in 250°F oven for about 20 minutes, or until it is warm.

Variation: If you're cooking over a campfire, you can mix all the ingredients and place in a covered skillet or soup pot, and then warm in the hot coals of your fire for about 15 minutes. But be sure to check that it is not overcooking or burning.

Remember, everything is cooked already when placed into the baking dish. You only want to warm it up before serving.

SERVES THREE.

NEW ZEALAND SPINACH (*Tetragonia tetragonioides,* formerly *Tetragonia expansa*)

New Zealand spinach is part of the Fig Marigold or Ice Plant family (Aizoaceae), which includes 130 genera and 2,500 species.

The *Tetragonia* genus contains about 50 species worldwide.

IDENTIFYING NEW ZEALAND SPINACH

This is a succulent, low-growing plant that is highly branched. The alternately arranged leaves are triangular-ovate, with an entire or undulate margin. The solitary yellow-green flowers are found in the axils.

New Zealand spinach, a native of Southeast Asia, has now naturalized along the West Coast. The succulent plant grows like ice plant, sprawling over sandy areas, salt marshes, and even gardens.

The plant can be successfully grown in gardens in warm climates, and because it is sensitive to frost, it should be grown in a greenhouse in colder climes.

USES

The tender tips of New Zealand spinach are collected and used just as you'd use common spinach.

The wild plant can be found all along the Pacific coast up to Oregon. It is a low-growing plant, about 3 to 5 inches tall, and is often found in large, rather dense mat-like patches. The tender tips can be pinched off and lightly seasoned with vinegar and oil. Adding avocado and tomato will result in a superb salad.

Mix the plant into potato salad, green salad, or coleslaw. The leaves make a good salad by themselves.

The leaves are tasty just lightly steamed. Or, as you'd use common spinach, add the leaves to soups, crepes, quiches, omelets, and mixed vegetable dishes.

New Zealand spinach leaves are more succulent and substantial than common spinach.

New Zealand spinach spreading wildly at the edge of an urban neighborhood garden.

New Zealand spinach growing on the beach at the Pacific Ocean.

Vacation at the Beach (a Salad)

3 cups New Zealand spinach leaves
½ red onion, diced
1 ripe tomato, diced
1 ripe avocado, sliced
1 minced garlic clove
1 tablespoon oil
1 tablespoon apple cider vinegar
1 teaspoon dill weed

A view of the succulent leaves of New Zealand spinach.

Collect the fresh New Zealand spinach leaves, rinse them, and put them in your salad bowl. Add the diced onion and diced tomato, the avocado slices, and the minced garlic clove. Add the oil, vinegar, and dill and toss well.

This salad is delicious served with a thick clam chowder (on a pier overlooking the beach, of course).

SERVES FOUR.

Summer's End

6 large Jerusalem artichokes (if unavailable, 2 large potatoes)
Butter (for skillet)
1 onion or a bunch of wild onions, diced
2 cups New Zealand spinach, cleaned and chopped
Garlic powder and powdered sage leaves, to taste

Slice the Jerusalem artichokes (or potatoes) into thin pieces and lay them into a hot, buttered cast-iron or stainless steel skillet. Sauté until almost thoroughly cooked, turning the slices occasionally so they won't burn. Add the onion(s) and cook for another 3 to 4 minutes. Now add the New Zealand spinach and cover the skillet. Let it cook until the greens are done.

For seasoning, try a dash of garlic powder and powdered sage leaves.

SERVES FOUR.

The tender tips of New Zealand spinach are being collected. They will be washed and added to an egg dish.

Winter Treat

5 cups New Zealand spinach leaves and tender stems
¼ cup dried seaweeds (sea lettuce, dulse, kelp, or your choice)
2 teaspoons lemon juice
4 tablespoons mayonnaise

Into a pot (for steaming or boiling), put the fresh New Zealand leaves and stems. Make sure all the stems are tender. Then add the seaweeds. Steam the New Zealand spinach and seaweed for about 5 minutes.

Mix together the lemon juice and the mayonnaise, and use this mixture as a topping for the cooked greens.

This makes an excellent side dish to fresh fish.

SERVES FIVE.

Island Brunch (a Favorite of Shining Bear)

Olive oil
1 large Jerusalem artichoke
2 cups of New Zealand spinach tender tops
2 eggs

Warm the cast-iron skillet with olive oil. Slice the Jerusalem artichoke thinly and cook for a minute or so. Add the greens and continue to cook at low heat for about a minute. Add the eggs and cook until done.

SERVES TWO.

OXALIS, SOUR GRASS, SHAMROCK, WOOD SORREL (*Oxalis* spp.)

Oxalis is a member of the Wood Sorrel or Oxalis family (Oxalidaceae). This family consists of five genera and about 880 species worldwide.

The *Oxalis* genus consists of about 500 to 950 species worldwide.

IDENTIFYING OXALIS

The leaves are trifoliate (i.e., with three leaflets). Each leaflet is heart-shaped, and has a midrib or midfold that closes or folds back at night. This is one of the plants commonly called "shamrock" in honor of Saint Patrick, who supposedly used it to teach the Trinity to the pre-Christian Irish. This is because each leaf is composed of three leaflets.

The leaf stems are long and succulent. The flower stalks are also stout and succulent. The flowers are white, yellow, red, or pink, with 10 stamens and five petals.

Found throughout the United States, often in wooded areas, oxalis grows to about 8 to 10 inches tall.

USES

When including wood sorrel leaves and stems in any recipe, remember that it is a very sour plant and should be used sparingly.

Wild oxalis in an untended garden patch.

Overall view of the oxalis plant in flower.

The plant adds a vinegar-like tartness to salads, and it can even be fermented like cabbage to produce a sort of wild sauerkraut.

The leaves and stems can be added to soups, stews, and vegetable broths. In moderation, it can also be used in mixed vegetable dishes.

Wood sorrel leaves and stems can be used like rhubarb in pies.

The stems of this plant are succulent and full of moisture. They make a pleasant trail nibble.

A pink-flowered species of oxalis, sometimes planted as a garden plant.

Wood Sorrel Soup

1 cup wood sorrel flower stalks and leaves
1 cup water
1 onion
1 garlic clove
1 Jerusalem artichoke
2 tablespoons soy or potato flour
4 cups milk
Pepper to taste

Tear the wood sorrel into small pieces and add to a soup pot with the water. FInely dice the onion and garlic and quarter the Jerusalem artichoke. Add onion, garlic, and artichoke to soup pot. Let this cook until the onion and Jerusalem artichoke are almost tender.

Blend the flour with a little milk to form a smooth gravy and slowly pour into the soup, stirring while you pour. Add the rest of the milk and a dash of pepper. Let simmer for about 10 minutes and then serve.

SERVES ABOUT SIX.

Log Cabin Broth

1 carrot, diced
1 onion, diced
1 bell pepper, diced
4 cups water
1 garlic clove, finely diced
1½ cups wood sorrel stems and leaves
½ cup tofu (soybean curd), diced
1 tablespoon basil
1 tablespoon tamari sauce
1 teaspoon kelp powder

Though most oxalis tubers are small, they are related to the oca of South America, which are widely cultivated as a food crop.

Add the diced carrot, onion, and bell pepper to the water and begin cooking at a low temperature. Add the diced garlic and the wood sorrel, the tofu, and all the seasonings. Let the broth simmer for about 30 minutes before serving.

Serve with a bowl of long-grain brown rice or wild rice.

SERVES FOUR.

Hobo Jungle Stew

1 potato
½ onion
1 cup oxalis leaves
½ cup sow thistle leaves
1 tomato, diced (optional)

Dice the potato and onion and put in a pot with a little water. Let simmer in a covered pot for about 15 minutes. Add the oxalis and sow thistle leaves and continue to let the ingredients simmer for another 10 minutes (or until the potatoes and onions are tender). The potatoes and onions can be substituted with Jerusalem artichokes and wild onion bulbs and leaves.

This is a pleasant vegetable dish without seasoning, but you may wish to add a dash of salt or powdered kelp. Also, one tomato, diced into small pieces, can be added to the pot about 5 minutes before it is done.

SERVES TWO.

PLANTAIN (*Plontago major, lanceolata,* and related species)

Plantain is a member of the Plantain family (Plantaginaceae). This family consists of about 110 genera and about 2,000 species worldwide.

The *Plantago* genus consists of about 250 species worldwide.

IDENTIFYING PLANTAIN

All of plantain's leaves are basal. The low-growing plants are often unnoticed in lawns and fields.

There are two most common species: narrowleaf plantain (*Plantago lanceolata*) and broadleaf plantain (*Plantago major*). Narrowleaf plantain's leaves are lance-shaped and prominently ribbed with parallel veins. Broadleaf plantain has a long leaf stalk and a round to ovate, glabrous leaf.

Flowers are formed in dense spikes on simple leafless stalks, each rising up to about 2 feet tall.

Plantains are as common as dandelions across the United States, but they are not generally recognized by name. The plant is found in lawns, gardens, marshes, swamps, disturbed soils, and agricultural lands throughout the United States.

By the way, this plantain is wholly unrelated to the *platano*, or banana, found in Mexico and elsewhere in the world. Only the name is the same.

USES

Tender young plantain leaves can be added to salads. However, as the plant matures, it becomes both bitter and fibrous. The fibers are prominent, similar

Broadleaf plantain. PHOTO BY RICK ADAMS.

Broadleaf plantain going to seed. PHOTO BY RICK ADAMS.

Narrowleaf plantain growing in a lawn.

A large broadleaf plantain leaf growing in a river bottom area.

to the fibers of celery, and somewhat tough. Therefore, older leaves should be steamed or stewed, after you've pulled out the most prominent veins.

The seeds can be easily harvested when the plant is mature. Once winnowed, the seeds can be soaked and cooked like rice.

Narrowleaf plantain growing in hard-packed soil along a wilderness trail.

Angelo Cervera collects seeds from the narrowleaf plantain.

Plantain Roll

Plantain leaves

STUFFING

1 pound ground beef
2 cups rice
1 garlic clove, diced
5 nasturtium leaves, finely diced
1 egg, beaten

This recipe is a variation of stuffed grape leaves. In this case, we'll simply be substituting plantain leaves for grape leaves.

First boil or steam the plantain leaves until they are tender. You may need to pull out the fibers on older leaves.

Cook the ground beef in a pan until lightly browned. Remove the grease. Cook the rice until tender, and then add the rice to the pan of ground beef. Add the garlic, nasturtium leaves, and egg and let cook until everything is tender.

Place a heaping tablespoon of the filling onto each plantain leaf and fold the leaf around the filling, tucking the seams underneath. Each roll will look like a fat cigar. Place the rolls in a baking dish and bake for about 15 minutes at 200°F—just long enough for rolls to warm up.

WILL MAKE ABOUT 20 ROLLS, MORE OR LESS.

Lunch in Ogalala (a Soup)

3 cups plantain leaves, finely diced
4 cups water or milk (OK to substitute almond milk)
1 turnip
1 Jerusalem artichoke
½ cup whole-wheat or potato flour
2 eggs (optional)
Pepper to taste

You may need to remove some of the tough fibers before preparing the leaves. Start the leaves simmering in the water or milk. Using milk results in a thicker, creamier soup. You can use powdered milk for this soup with acceptable results. If you use milk, do not let the soup boil—make sure that it only simmers.

Chop up the turnip and Jerusalem artichoke and add to the soup. In a cup, slowly add water to the flour and stir until you get a sauce with an even consistency. Add this to the soup, all the while stirring so no lumps form. Separate the egg yolks from the whites and beat each separately. Slowly add the yolks, all the while stirring. Next add the whites, continually stirring. Add pepper to taste, and serve when the roots are tender.

SERVES FIVE.

Hahamongna Swamp Salad

1 cup tender plantain leaves
1 cup cattail shoots
½ cup dock leaves
½ cup watercress leaves
½ cup wild onions (bulb and leaves)

DRESSING

1 tablespoon vinegar
1 tablespoon oil

Make certain the plantain leaves are not too bitter or fibrous for salad. The cattail shoots are the lower section of the tender stalks, peeled back to the nonfibrous tender white insides. Dice this section along with the plantain, dock, and watercress and add to the salad bowl. Dice the onions once the fibrous parts have been removed. (You can substitute homegrown or store-bought onions if you aren't able to find any in the wild. Make sure that any wild onion you collect has that typical onion aroma or don't eat it.) Add the dressing and toss well.

SERVES FIVE.

PRICKLY PEAR CACTUS (*Opuntia* spp.)

Prickly pear is a member of the Cactus family (Cactaceae). The Cactus family contains about 125 genera and 1,800 species worldwide.

The *Opuntia* genus contains about 150 species.

IDENTIFYING PRICKLY PEAR CACTUS

Prickly pear cactus is easily recognized by its flat, broad, oval, fleshy pads covered with numerous spines. The colorful flowers are followed by the fruits, which resemble small oblong apples. The fruits, which form on the tips of the pads, are full of seeds.

Prickly pear cactus is found throughout the United States, primarily in the Southwest, but also as far east as Nebraska, and some are even found along the Atlantic coast. The plant prefers arid environments. Prickly pear cactus can grow to the size of a shrub, 4 to 5 feet tall, or it can be pruned tree-like, up to 10 feet tall.

The young, tender prickly pear cactus pad (or "nopal").

USES

The older prickly pear pads are fibrous and woody and are generally not used for food. Only the younger, still glossy green new growth is used. Pick these young pads carefully with gloves or a brown paper bag to protect the hands from spines and the tiny glochids at the base of each spine.

A good source of moisture, one of these young pads can be picked, peeled, and eaten raw. The flavor is mildly sour and reminiscent of green pepper.

A view of the ripe prickly pear cactus fruit (or "tuna").

The raw pads can be peeled and diced and included in most green salads.

The diced pads are commonly cooked with eggs and onions in omelets. The peeled pads can be sliced thin and sautéed with onions and tomatoes. Or the diced pads can be added to soups, stews, and baked vegetable dishes.

The purple, red, orange, or yellow fruits are sweet and delicious. They need only be carefully picked, their spines and glochids removed, then peeled and eaten. To safely pick, I use metal salad tongs and carefully twist off each fruit.

Diann Benti with a young prickly pear cactus pad.

The glochids are scraped from the surface of the pad with a flat knife.

The edge of the pad is removed.

A view of the uncleaned pad (left) and the cleaned pad (right), ready to prepare for eating.

Diann Benti shows the cleaned pad, ready to eat.

Then, using the metal tongs again, I hold each fruit over a flame for about 5 seconds, turning the fruit to burn off all the glochids. Then I can brush or wash the surface of the fruits. Finally, each fruit is cut in half, and the edible fruit is easily removed from the thicker rind.

The fruits are commonly made into candy, pies, jams, drinks, and various dessert items.

Cleaned cactus pads, sliced and ready to be gently sautéed.

A student cleans and chops the cactus pads to prepare for cooking.

End of Summer Salad

1 cup young cactus pads, peeled and diced
1 cup tomatoes, diced
1 avocado, peeled and sliced
1 onion or ½ cup wild onion greens, finely chopped
¼ head lettuce or 1 cup young sow thistle leaves
1 teaspoon oil
1 tablespoon vinegar
Kelp powder, dill, and garlic powder to taste

Combine all the ingredients and season. Note the versatility of this recipe, depending on which plants are available or in season.

Note: Some people find the raw pads a bit too mucilaginous to be palatable, especially when used in salads. There are a few ways to reduce the "sliminess" of the cactus pads. One method is to peel the cactus and lay the pads on paper towels for a bit, so the paper absorbs some of the moisture. Then dice and add the cactus to the salad. Another method is to peel and slice the cactus, and boil it. Much of the mucilaginous quality can be boiled out. Then the cactus is placed on paper towels to drain. It then can be added to salads, though it would be better if first chilled.

SERVES TWO.

Palm Canyon Cactus Casserole

12 boiled Jerusalem artichokes or 6 boiled potatoes, diced
5 cactus pads, peeled and diced
2 eggs
2 onions, diced
½ stick butter
Kelp, dill weed, pepper, and garlic powder to taste
1½ cups cheddar cheese, grated

Combine all the ingredients, except the cheese, in a baking dish. Bake in an oven for 1 hour at 200°F. Cover with the cheese when still hot, just before serving. If an oven is not available (because you're camping, or because the gas lines are severed or cut off), this casserole can be baked in a container with a tight-fitting lid by placing the container in a bed of coals (for about the same amount of time). This casserole can also be baked in a solar cooker, either a reflector-type oven or a "hot box"–type solar cooker.

SERVES FIVE.

Desert Delectable (an Omelet)

2 cups prickly pear cactus pads, peeled and diced
Butter
2 cups onions, diced
6 eggs, beaten

Once the pads are peeled and diced, place them in a heated and buttered frying pan. Sauté at a low temperature, and add the diced onions in 5 minutes. Continue to sauté until the cactus changes in color from bright green to a dull green, almost browned. Add the eggs and cook omelet-style.

Serve with a warm tortilla and either a pickled jalapeño chile or a pickled kelp bladder.

SERVES THREE.

Basic Sustenance

2 cups prickly pear cactus pads, peeled and diced
Butter
1 cup onions, diced
Garlic powder to taste
Miso powder to taste

Sauté the peeled and diced cactus in butter in a cast-iron skillet. Cook until the bright green color changes to a greenish-brown color. This change in color indicates that the water has been largely cooked off. Add onions and cook until they are tender. Season with garlic powder and miso, and serve as the vegetable alongside your main dish, or as the main meal if nothing else is available.

Due to the widespread availability of cactus pads, and the availability of wild or domestic onions, this is a good dish that can be prepared under most circumstances, either out in the backcountry or in the city.

SERVES TWO.

Students gather around the cooking cactus pads and other wild foods.

Breaded Cactus Pad

Several young, tender prickly pear cactus pads

BATTER

1 cup whole-wheat flour
3 eggs
⅓ cup milk
1 teaspoon garlic salt
1 teaspoon kelp powder
¼ teaspoon powdered basil
Oil (for frying)

Anthropologist Paul Campbell watches the prickly pear cactus cook as he prepares another pan.

Carefully peel the young cactus pads, being certain to remove all the spines and glochids. Slice each pad into thin segments, then boil or steam all the cactus slices. The water will get extremely mucilaginous. Rinse the cactus slices in cold water to remove some of the sliminess. Lay the cactus slices on a cloth so that some of the moisture can be absorbed from the cactus. This will help the batter adhere to the cactus.

Blend all the batter ingredients together in a bowl.

Heat the oil in your frying pan. Dip each cactus slice into the batter, and then place it into the hot oil. Let cook until each slice is golden brown. This is best served immediately, but you can keep it warm in your oven or in a covered pot near your campfire.

I enjoy this as is, but for seasoning suggestions, try lemon juice sprinkled on each slice, or good-quality tomato ketchup (possibly made from your own garden tomatoes), or even a dash of mustard (without the yellow dye).

MAKES ABOUT A DOZEN SERVINGS.

Enrique Villaseñor in front of a patch of prickly pear cactus.

MEET ENRIQUE VILLASEÑOR:
AMBASSADOR OF THE PRICKLY PEAR CACTUS

Enrique Villaseñor is at the head of the classroom, extolling the many unsung virtues of the prickly pear cactus. "It's often referred to as poor people's food," he explains, "but did you know that it contains all the essential amino acids, and some non-essential amino acids as well?" Villaseñor is the de facto ambassador of the humble prickly pear cactus, a plant that has been used for food and medicine for millennia.

Enrique Villaseñor with cleaned cactus fruits.

After 35 years as a schoolteacher, Villaseñor recently retired and now actively works as an assistant to pharmacologist Dr. James Adams, who shares traditional Chumash healing methods.

In the 2-hour presentation, Villaseñor takes his audience through the fascinating history, and the vast healthful benefits, of the prickly pear cactus, beginning with the fact that cacti remnants were found in jars in Mexico dating back 10,000 years. He explains that archaeologists have found old jars that contained not only cactus, but teosinte (the forerunner to corn), chili, amaranth, sapote, and mesquite, some of the earliest foods from this continent.

"The prickly pear cactus is one of the best immune system boosters," says Villaseñor, quoting Hippocrates, who said, "Let food be thy medicine, and let medicine be thy food."

Historically, prickly pear cactus pads have been used for lowering cholesterol levels, digestive issues, edema, wounds, bronchitis, fevers, vitiligo, inflammation, type II diabetes, muscle pain, urinary problems, burns, and liver problems. Students of Villaseñor listen in awe, wondering why they have always considered the prickly pear just as a food to eat when you're next to starving, rather than the superfood it is.

Enrique Villaseñor blends a batch of "Agua de Nopales" for the students to taste.

The highlight of Villaseñor's presentation is when he turns on a food processor and makes a prickly pear drink for everyone to try. Everyone enjoys the tartness and sweetness of the drink. No sugar is ever added.

THE RECIPE

"Agua de Nopales"—Prickly Pear Cactus Water, by Enrique Villaseñor

1 prickly pear cactus pad (cleaned and rinsed)
2 cups of chilled water
1 green apple
1 peeled orange
Ice
Lime to taste

Dice the prickly pear pad. Place in blender with 2 cups of water. Blend. Dice the green apple. Blend. Dice the peeled orange. Blend. Add additional water to taste if the smoothie is too thick for you. Serve chilled with ice. Use lime to taste. Do not add sugar. Suggested serving is 1½ cups twice a day. Enjoy!

According to Villaseñor, this is one of the best ways to get your daily intake of the prickly pear, in a form that is tasty and easy to prepare. It strengthens your immune system, helps you to lose weight, and lowers your cholesterol.

Enrique Villaseñor can be contacted at Senornopales@gmail.comñ

Prickly Pear Ice Cream

10 ripe cactus fruits
1 gallon milk

Carefully peel the cactus fruits, being careful not to get the tiny spines in your skin. You can remove the seeds, or not. The seeds are small and you can just chew them up. They add character to the final product. However, you will notice the seeds. So, if you wish to remove them, here's an easy way. Put the peeled fruit into a blender and blend. Then pour the pulp through a sieve, which should effectively remove all the seeds.

Put the fruit pulp (either strained or unstrained) and milk into an ice-cream maker, electric or hand-crank, and proceed to make ice cream. Another method is to simply mix together the milk (or, better yet, cream) and the thoroughly mashed fruit pulp, and put it into your freezer. In approximately 2 hours, you'll have a product resembling ice cream.

MAKES ABOUT FOUR SERVINGS.

PURSLANE (*Portulaca oleracea*)

Purslane is a member of the Purslane family (Portulacaceae). This family contains only one genus, *Portulaca*, with about 100 species worldwide.

IDENTIFYING PURSLANE

Purslane sprawls along the ground with its fleshy, succulent, highly branched stems. The stems are round and tinted red. The flavor of the raw stems is mild and slightly sour, and the texture is crunchy.

The leaves are paddle-shaped (obovate), flat, and alternately arranged.

The small flowers are yellow, sessile, and contain five two-lobed petals. The small seed capsules produce abundant black seeds.

Purslane grows all over the world, usually in disturbed soil. It is often found in rose beds, gardens, and in the sandy soil of riparian areas.

USES

Purslane is a succulent, low-growing plant that is very tasty and crunchy. The entire plant can be used, the stems being most succulent.

Purslane can be used as the main salad ingredient, lightly seasoned with diced onion, vinegar, and oil.

The plant is good cooked with soups, steamed, sautéed, or pickled. Add it to omelets, too.

The sprawling purslane plant.

The entire above-ground plant can be eaten. The thick succulent stems also make a great pickle.

Thoreau used and enjoyed purslane, and he wrote of the plant: "I have made a satisfactory dinner off a dish of purslane which I gathered and boiled. Yet men have come to such a pass that they frequently starve, not from want of necessaries, but for want of luxuries."

Traveler's Joy (a Wild Salad)

3 cups purslane
1 cup chickweed
½ cup amaranth leaves
½ onion (wild, if available)
1 ripe avocado
1 hard-boiled egg, sliced
Approximately ¼ cup swiss cheese, diced into small bits
Juice of ½ lemon
1 teaspoon garlic salt

Much of this salad can be gathered on the trail (and maybe in your own backyard).

Chop the purslane, chickweed, amaranth, and onion into bite-size bits. Peel and dice the avocado and add it to the mixture. Add the hard-boiled egg. Mix in approximately ¼ cup of swiss cheese. Squeeze the lemon over the salad, add the garlic salt, and mix well. If you have them, you can add chia seeds and even a tablespoon of mayonnaise to this lip-smacking salad.

MAKES FIVE MEDIUM SERVINGS.

Verdolago con Queso

1 quart purslane, including stems
Approximately ½ cup Monterey jack cheese, shredded

Collect tender purslane, including the stems, and carefully rinse to remove any sand or soil. Gently boil for about 2 minutes or until tender. Drain the water and chop the purslane into smaller pieces. Return the purslane to the frying pan and shred the jack cheese over it. Keep the purslane in the pan just until the cheese melts. Be careful not to overmelt the cheese.

Serve warm.

SERVES TWO.

Pickled Purslane

1 quart purslane stems and leaves
3 garlic cloves, sliced
10 peppercorns
1 quart apple cider vinegar (or old pickle juice, jalapeño pepper juice, etc.)

Clean the purslane stems and leaves by rinsing with fresh water. Cut into 1-inch pieces and place in clean jars with lids. Add the spices and pour the vinegar over the purslane. Keep this in the refrigerator and wait at least 2 weeks before using.

Serve as a side dish with omelets and sandwiches.

Verdolago con Huevos

2 cups purslane, with stems, diced
1 cup wild or domestic onion, or 1 cup nasturtium leaves and stems, diced
Butter
6 eggs, beaten

Carefully clean and rinse the purslane. The entire above-ground plant can be used as long as it is still tender. Add the diced onion and purslane to a heated and buttered cast-iron skillet. Cook for about 5 minutes. Add the eggs and cook omelet-style.

Serve with a tomato slice.

SERVES THREE.

Bundles of purslane are sold alongside other vegetables at this farmers' market.

Ranch-Style Purslane

Approximately 1 cup of purslane growing tips
Flour
Beaten eggs
Fine bread crumbs
Olive oil or butter, as needed

Collect the tender new tips of purslane—about the last 2 or 3 inches of the stems. Rinse these in water to remove any sand. Roll them (or shake them) in flour until thoroughly coated, and then dip in the beaten eggs. Next, cover each purslane stalk with bread crumbs. This process is easiest to do if you simply line up the three dishes of flour, eggs, and bread crumbs and do the breading production line–style.

When the breading is done, fry or sauté each purslane stalk for about 5 minutes or until golden brown in olive oil or butter. Serve with tartar sauce, mustard, or sour cream. This is a unique hors d'oeuvre for even your finest parties.

SERVES ABOUT FOUR.

Ham and Purslane on Rye (a Delectable Sandwich)

2 slices rye bread, toasted or untoasted
A few slices good-quality ham
A handful of fresh purslane, stems included
Mustard/horseradish mix

Layer ingredients per usual and enjoy. Instead of lettuce or pickles on this ham sandwich, you're using fresh purslane. It's quite flavorful. The slightly crunchy flavor of the crisp, succulent purslane stems helps to make this a satisfying sandwich.

SERVES ONE.

Recipe submitted by Greg Kirshner, Fullerton, California.

RUSSIAN THISTLE (*Salsola kali*)

Russian thistle is a member of the Goosefoot family (Chenopodiaceae). The Goosefoot family includes 100 genera and 1,500 species worldwide.

There are about 100 species of *Salsola* worldwide.

IDENTIFYING RUSSIAN THISTLE

Russian thistle, when mature, is the commonly recognized tumbleweed of the Plains and Southwest. The plant begins grass-like, all the spiny needle-like leaves arising from each root. The plant grows taller and gradually develops into a ball. The root of the mature plant is easily broken and the plant is carried for long distances by the winds, distributing seeds along the way.

Russian thistle can grow up to 5 feet tall, but more commonly it reaches about 3 feet. It grows primarily in compacted soil.

A view of the Russian thistle stems and leaves. Note the red in the axils.

USES

This is a true "survival food." During the Great Depression when no other food was available to people of the Plains, people stayed alive by eating cooked Russian thistle.

The Russian thistle plant in a field as it matures, going to seed. At this stage, only the tender tips can be collected for food. PHOTO BY RICK ADAMS.

Russian thistle can be eaten only if it is collected young enough. When the new sprouts are emerging, the plant appears almost grass-like—a bluish-green type of tough grass. The young sprouts can be cut and steamed or sautéed to make a delicious cooked vegetable. Seasoned with butter, these are most tasty.

The plant could be used in salads if it is chopped fine, but it usually is not considered a salad plant. This is because the raw plant can cause irritation in the throat due to its prickliness.

A view of the needle-like segments of the Russian thistle leaves.

From an older plant, if it hasn't completely dried up and matured into a rolling, tumbling ball, you still might be able to pinch off some tender green tips and steam them. These won't be as tender as the young shoots, but they can be used if other foods are not available.

Tumbled Rice

1 cup rice
4 cups Russian thistle
1 cup black mustard leaves and tender stems
1 teaspoon pepper
1 teaspoon garlic powder
Approximately ⅓ cup jack cheese, shredded

Begin by cooking the rice. Wild rice would be ideal; otherwise, use long-grain brown rice.

Use only the tenderest portions of the Russian thistle leaves and stalk. In a separate pot, steam the Russian thistle for about 3 minutes before adding the mustard greens. If the mustard is tender enough, use tender stem sections also.

If your timing is right, both the rice and the greens will be done at the same time. Mix both together and season with the pepper and garlic powder.

Serve hot, with a sprinkle of the shredded jack cheese over the top.

SERVES FIVE.

Lean Greens (Steamed Russian Thistle)

2 cups very young Russian thistle tips
Butter
Salt to taste

Collect the very young, still tender Russian thistle stems. Those that are not fibrous and still edible will easily snap off when bent. When very young, most of the above-ground plant can be collected and used. When older, only the tender growing tips can be used.

The plant loses very little bulk when cooked. Rinse the tender growing tips and then steam them. If desired, cut the steamed plant into smaller, bite-size pieces.

Season with butter and serve with a piece of whole-wheat toast.

SERVES TWO.

Tumbleweed Broth

5 cups water, seasoned (to taste) with miso
1 potato (Jerusalem artichoke can be used)
1 onion (wild onion bulbs and greens can be used)
3 garlic cloves
2 cups Russian thistle leaves and tender stems
½ cup watercress, chopped
¼ cup parsley, chopped
1 bay leaf

No longer edible, this Russian thistle "tumbleweed" rolled into town after a wind.

Dice the potato into small pieces. Simmer the potato in the miso-seasoned broth. (You can substitute a Jerusalem artichoke for the potato.) Dice one large onion or chop at least 1 cup of wild onion bulbs and leaves. Add to broth. Peel and slice the garlic cloves and add them as well. Now, making sure you've only collected the tender portions of the Russian thistle, cut it all into small pieces about 1 inch in length. Add all the Russian thistle to the broth.

Next, add the watercress and parsley to the pot. Add the bay leaf and let the mixture simmer for about 20 minutes—at least until the potatoes are well cooked.

Served with one of the salads described in this book, this makes an excellent wintry-day lunch.

SERVES FOUR.

SHEPHERD'S PURSE (*Capsella bursa-pastoris*)

Shepherd's purse is a member of the Mustard family (Brassicaceae). The Mustard family is another large family, comprising more than 330 genera worldwide and about 3,780 species.

The *Capsella* genus contains four species.

IDENTIFYING SHEPHERD'S PURSE

Shepherd's purse is often an inconspicuous weed, growing in grass, fields, and disturbed soils across the country. The majority of the leaves are basal. These are deeply incised with a large terminal lobe. The leaves are sparsely covered with stiff bristle-like hairs. The leaves appearing on the flower stalk are stalkless and clasp the stem in an arrowhead fashion. The flower stalk leaves are generally untoothed.

The flower stalks rise up to 2 feet tall, but generally average about a foot tall. The fruits are most conspicuous since they are distinctly heart-shaped.

A view of the heart-shaped seed pods of shepherd's purse.

This shepherd's purse is arising from a field of chickweed.

USES

Shepherd's purse is a pleasant-tasting member of the Mustard family, which is found across the entire United States. The leaves are tender and can be used as a main salad ingredient; the leaves that grow on the flower stalk are smaller and typically sparse.

The plant is usually recognized by its most conspicuous, heart-shaped fruits. The leaves can be pinched off (no need to uproot the plant), rinsed, and added to your salad bowl. The mild pepperiness of the leaves is enhanced by a light vinegar and oil dressing, a pinch of kelp, and a diced garlic clove. Or you might enjoy a simple dressing of a freshly squeezed lemon over your shepherd's purse salad.

Shepherd's purse leaves can be used in most any salad recipe. Mix them into salads of garden lettuce, spinach, or various wild greens, and use such foods as avocado, tomato, hard-boiled eggs, and tuna to enhance the salads.

The leaves can be simply steamed or sautéed with onions, and served with butter. A dish of steamed shepherd's purse leaves is just right with baked rainbow trout and hot bay tea.

The main difficulty with shepherd's purse is not in finding ways to use it but in finding enough of it. Although the leaves are sometimes quite large (in the early spring, in rich soil), they are usually relatively small. Therefore, unless you've located a solid stand of the plant, it may take some time and effort to collect enough leaves for a large salad.

Shepherd's Repast

2 cups shepherd's purse leaves
2 cups chickweed
½ to 1 cup wild onions
2 tablespoons olive oil (if available)
1 lemon
Dash salt and/or pepper

Here's a salad that is easy to prepare in the early spring when you're out exploring the wilderness, tending sheep, or even if you're just at home in the city.

Collect the early spring greens, rinse them, and tear into bite-size pieces. Add the wild onions, greens and bulbs, diced into bite-size pieces. Now you're ready for the seasoning.

Simple is best in this case, since we want to be able to taste the subtle and delicious flavor of the wild greens. Add olive oil and squeeze the juice of a lemon over the salad. Add salt and/or pepper to taste, and then your salad is ready.

SERVES FOUR.

The young leaves of shepherd's purse.

Feast of the Vagabond (an Omelet)

½ onion
Olive oil or butter, as needed
3 eggs, beaten
1 cup fresh, rinsed shepherd's purse leaves
Chile peppers

Mince ½ an onion and sauté it at a low heat with olive oil or butter. Use your small cast-iron skillet that you carry in your vagabond's knapsack.

When the onions are tender, add the eggs and cover the skillet. When the eggs are about half-cooked, fold in the leaves of shepherd's purse. Let the omelet cook at low heat until done.

This simple dish will be even more enjoyable if you can serve it with a chile pepper.

Although this recipe was done with store-bought bulb onions, you can substitute wild green onions for a much "fresher" flavor.

If your chicken isn't laying, then use your shepherd's purse leaves and onion for salad.

SERVES TWO.

The Eagle Soars at Noon (a Simple Stew)

2 large golden potatoes
1 large onion (or 1 cup wild onions)
5 cups water
1 bay leaf
1 cup shepherd's purse leaves, rinsed
2 tablespoons chia seeds
Seaweed or powdered kelp, to taste
Dr. Bronner's Liquid Aminos, to taste

Dice the potatoes and onions and begin by simmering them in the water. Wild onions are preferred (all fibrous parts removed), and Jerusalem artichokes can be substituted for the potatoes. Add the bay leaf to the soup.

When the potatoes and onions are almost tender, add the rinsed shepherd's purse leaves, the chia, and kelp. Let simmer until done.

This simple stew can be served with fresh fruit and bread such as sourdough, or a tortilla.

As you rest and enjoy this lunchtime repast, raise your sights; see the eagle in flight, soaring in the clouds.

SERVES FIVE.

SOW THISTLE (*Sonchus oleraceus*)

Sow thistle is a member of the Sunflower family (Asteraceae). The Sunflower family has about 1,500 genera and about 23,000 species. This is one of the largest botanical families. Botanist Jepson divides this very large family into 14 groups. All plants addressed here from the Sunflower family are within "Group 8"(the Chicory Tribe), described as having ligulate heads, five-lobed ligules (five teeth per petal), and generally containing milky sap when broken.

The *Sonchus* genus contains about 55 species worldwide.

IDENTIFYING SOW THISTLE

Sow thistle resembles dandelion, but there are a few important differences. While dandelion's leaves are all basal, with only one flower per stalk, sow thistle's leaves appear both on the flower stalk and at ground level. Sow thistle's flower stalks have many flowers per stalk. Dandelion is a low-growing plant, but sow thistle grows to approximately 4 feet tall—and taller in ideal conditions.

Sow thistle is a common weed throughout the entire United States. It's found in gardens, vacant lots, orchards, fields, lawns, and wilderness areas.

The plant is commonly confused with the closely related dandelion.

A bee collecting sow thistle nectar.

A flowering sow thistle plant. The individual flowers are very similar to dandelion flowers.

A young sow thistle plant.

The newly emerging sow thistle plant of spring, surrounded by a bed of chickweed.

This sow thistle plant is just starting to flower.

USES

Young sow thistle leaves are mild-flavored and have a texture similar to garden lettuce. If the plant hasn't become bitter yet, it can be prepared as a main salad ingredient. A light seasoning (vinegar, oil, garlic) is all that's needed, but you might want to add avocado, onion, tomato, other wild greens, and so on. Try a dressing of blue cheese or mayonnaise for a most flavorful salad.

When the plant is older, it becomes slightly bitter. At this stage it is best steamed. Cook it with onions and other greens and season lightly.

Sow thistle leaves can be added to soups, omelets, and stewed vegetable dishes. The tender sow thistle stems are pleasant to chew on, like celery, once peeled of their slightly fibrous outer skin. These tender stems can also be steamed or boiled, and topped with butter or cheese and served like asparagus.

Two relatives of sow thistle, dandelion and chicory, have roots that are commonly used as coffee substitutes when roasted. Sow thistle's root is generally smaller than that of dandelion or chicory, but it can still be used for this hearty coffee-like root beverage.

The individual flowers of sow thistle are yellow and resemble dandelion flowers.

Sow thistle leaves are more tender than dandelion leaves, and their color is almost bluish-green, compared to the darker green of dandelion.

Sow thistle is an annual, whereas dandelion is a perennial.

Vegetarian Sow Burger

2 cups cooked lentils
½ onion, boiled and finely diced
1 egg
2 tablespoons whole-wheat flour
1 teaspoon garlic powder
2 cups sow thistle leaves
Oil

Approximately 1 cup of uncooked lentils will yield about 2 cups when cooked. To the cooked lentils add ½ onion. Add the raw egg, flour, and garlic powder. Measure 2 cups of sow thistle leaves, firmly packed, into a measuring cup. (If you're camping, a typical sierra cup measures almost exactly 1 cup.) Steam the sow thistle and then chop it fine before adding it to the other ingredients.

Mix all the ingredients well. You should be able to form patties that hold together well. If they don't hold together, you can add a little more flour and maybe some oil. Once you've formed the patties, sauté them in oil in a cast-iron skillet.

Serve with gently fried potato or Jerusalem artichoke segments. Don't forget the sassafras tea.

YIELDS SIX MEDIUM-SIZED BURGERS.

Sow Thistle à la Carte

3 cups sow thistle leaves and tender stems
Butter
½ onion

Collect the tender sow thistle leaves and some of the tender stems. The stems, as they get older, may need to be peeled of a slightly fibrous outer layer.

Put a little butter in a cast-iron frying pan and heat the pan. Add the sow thistle, torn into bite-size pieces, and lay onion slices on top of the sow thistle. Cover the pan and let the mixture cook at low heat until the sow thistle is wilted and the thinly sliced onions are tender.

Serve with a thin slice of butter on top.

SERVES TWO (OR ONE HUNGRY HIKER).

Sonchus Salad

3 cups tender young sow thistle leaves
1 cup freshly picked loose-leaf garden lettuce (or use 1 cup wild mustard leaves)
2 tomatoes, diced into bite-size pieces
2 hard-boiled eggs, sliced
2 tablespoons oil
2 tablespoons vinegar or lemon juice
1 teaspoon pepper

Taste the sow thistle to be certain it has not become bitter. Rinse the leaves, tear into bite-size pieces, and put them in a salad bowl. Pick 1 cup of garden lettuce. (If you're camping in the backcountry, substitute 1 cup of mustard greens.) Add the two tomatoes and the hard-boiled egg slices. Finally, add your dressing: oil, vinegar or lemon juice, and pepper.

Mix well and breathe deeply as you enjoy this life-sustaining food.

SERVES FOUR.

Sow Thistle Scramble

6 eggs
3 cups sow thistle, chopped fine
⅓ cup parsley or watercress, chopped
½ green pepper, chopped
6 green onions (ideally, freshly gathered wild onions), diced
1 prickly pear cactus pad, peeled and diced (be careful not to get the spines and glochids in your skin)

TOPPING

Jalapeño peppers (or pickled kelp bladders)
Hot sauce

Begin by breaking all the eggs into a mixing bowl. Vigorously beat all the eggs. Add the chopped sow thistle leaves and parsley (or watercress) to the eggs. Add the green pepper, onions, and the prickly pear cactus pad. Mix all the ingredients together and then pour into an oiled and heated frying pan. Mix while cooking, as you'd cook scrambled eggs.

Serve with a splash of hot sauce and one jalapeño pepper (sliced or whole, as you wish) on each dish.

The perfect companion to such a breakfast would be caffeine-free sow thistle root "coffee" (see recipe on the next page).

SERVES FOUR.

Sow Thistle Coffee

This beverage is made from the larger roots of sow thistle in the same way that you'd make either dandelion or chicory root coffee. The roots are dug, carefully cleaned, and then laid in the sun or placed in the oven to dry. When the roots are completely dry (test the degree of dryness by breaking a root in two), grind them to a coarse powder in a grain or seed grinder. Either high-tech or low-tech can be used for grinding: Use a coffee grinder or use a flat rock. Now return the roots to the oven and roast the powder until it becomes dark brown—but be careful not to burn it! Roasting can also be accomplished by placing the powder in a thin layer in a pan over the coals of a campfire. Shake the pan occasionally so no burning occurs.

Once the roots are roasted, they can be used. Using a simple drip coffeemaker, measure about 1 teaspoon of the powder per cup. Pour the boiling water over the grounds and let your sow thistle beverage drip into your cup. This "coffee" can be drunk as is, or flavored with honey and/or cream.

Sow thistle, dandelion, and chicory roots have all been used as coffee extenders, usually during times of economic hardship, war, and famine when regular coffee is not readily available or only available in limited supplies.

I knew a man who regularly used sow thistle coffee during a period of unemployment. The plants were abundant in his backyard. He made a beverage from the roots, and he also steamed the leaves. His meals were rounded out with potatoes cooked in his fireplace.

VIOLET (*Viola* spp.)

Violet is a member of the Violet family (Violaceae). This family contains 23 genera and 830 species.

The *Viola* genus contains about 500 species.

IDENTIFYING VIOLET

Violet leaves are variable in shape, but they are commonly heart-shaped, on short-to-long stems (depending on species). The flowers can be white, yellow, pink, rose, or the most characteristic, violet-purple. The flowers appear solitary on stalks that are usually long. These perennials are found throughout the United States and have a wide variety of habitats, but generally prefer shady and moist places.

The common English violet, widely planted in gardens, is one of the best violets from the forager's viewpoint.

All the violet leaves can be eaten.

USES

The young leaves can be added to salads, usually mixed with other greens. Older greens develop a mild astringency, and they are best cooked, either alone as steamed greens or mixed with other greens or vegetables.

Violets can be added to soups and egg dishes.

Violet in the wild (*Viola adunca*). PHOTO BY JEAN PAWEK.

Violet leaves can be used in salads or cooked in a steamer. PHOTO BY JEAN PAWEK.

Jam can also be made with the flowers, using a standard jam recipe. The difficult part is collecting enough flowers to make jam.

Violette (an Omelet)

Butter, as needed
4 eggs
2 cups violet greens, washed and finely chopped
½ cup lamb's-quarters greens, finely chopped
1 garlic clove
Salt/pepper to taste

Melt the butter in a cast-iron skillet. Break the eggs into a mixing bowl and add the violet greens and the lamb's-quarters greens. Beat the eggs with the violet and lamb's-quarters greens and pour into the heated skillet.

While it's all cooking at low heat, chop up the garlic clove very fine and add it to the egg mixture in the skillet. Let the omelet cook until it's reached the desired consistency. Fold in half, let cook a little longer, and serve. Season with a dash of salt and/or pepper.

SERVES TWO.

Fruits, Roots, and Shoots at the Treestump Cafe (a Salad)

1 cup young violet leaves
1 cup miner's lettuce
½ cup cattail shoots
1 apple, diced
1 pear, diced
4 toothwort tubers (or 2 large radishes)
¼ cup raisins (approximately)
Juice of ½ lemon
Pinch of dill weed and salt

Tear the violet leaves and miner's lettuce into bite-size pieces and place in a salad bowl. Once you've removed all the fibrous outer layers of the cattail shoots, dice the tender insides and add to the salad. Add the diced apple and pear to the salad bowl. Dig up the toothwort tubers, wash them well, slice thin, and add to the salad. If toothwort is unavailable, use two fresh radishes instead. Add the raisins.

Squeeze the lemon juice over the salad and add a pinch of dill weed and salt. For variety, you can add either sour cream, cream cheese, or unflavored yogurt to this salad.

Enjoy this salad at the "Treestump Cafe." In this unique restaurant, the entertainment consists of dancing squirrels and singing blue jays. Be sure to leave a tip.

SERVES FOUR.

Via de Santa Rosa

4 cups violet leaves
1 cup lamb's-quarters leaves

Collect the violet leaves and remove any stems that are becoming coarse. You can use any of the lamb's-quarters plant that is still tender—stems and leaves. Put the leaves in a steamer and cook for about 10 minutes.

Serve plain, or with a bit of butter and a shake of kelp.

SERVES TWO.

The Howling Wind

1 Jerusalem artichoke or potato, diced
Milk (okay to use powdered or almond milk)
2 garlic cloves
1 cup violet greens, stems removed if fibrous
1 cup miner's lettuce
1 cup lamb's-quarters leaves
Dash of paprika
Dash of pepper

Add a diced Jerusalem artichoke or potato to your stew pot with just enough milk to cover so it can simmer. Add the two garlic cloves. Simmer at low heat, but do not boil.

When the potato or Jerusalem artichoke is almost tender, add the violet, miner's lettuce, and lamb's-quarters leaves, torn into bite-size pieces. Add paprika and pepper to season. Let simmer until all the leaves are cooked.

Serve warm with a piece of toast.

SERVES FOUR.

WATERCRESS (*Nasturtium officinale*)

Watercress is a member of the Mustard family (Brassicaceae). The Mustard family is another large family, comprising more than 330 genera worldwide and about 3,780 species.

The *Nasturtium* genus contains five species worldwide.

IDENTIFYING WATERCRESS

Watercress will almost always be found in slow-moving water. Occasionally it is found in very moist, sandy soil, such as along the edges of rivers and streams that have retreated during the summer.

The leaves are smooth and hairless, and are pinnately divided into roundish leaflets, with a larger single leaflet at the tip. The stalks of watercress are typically ⅛ inch to ¼ inch in diameter (even thicker in older plants). The stalks are hollow, and sometimes streaked with red pigment. The white roots are often visible at the bottom of the stalk.

The small (¼-inch-diameter) flowers are grouped in clusters called racemes. These flowers are arranged in the typical "mustard pattern."

All mustards, including watercress, have four petals in a cross or X shape. Although the petal colors for mustards vary, watercress flowers are always white. Under the petals, you'll always find four (usually green) sepals. Inside the petals, look for the six stamens (two short, four tall), and the one pistil in the middle. All mustards have this floral pattern. With this floral description firmly lodged in your memory, you can safely sample any plant that fits this description wherever you are over the entire face of the globe!

A view of the pinnately divided leaves of the watercress plant, growing in a stream.

Watercress growing along the edge of a stream.

Watercress in flower. PHOTO BY HELEN WONG.

Watercress is an ideal plant to know, since the forager can collect it not only in any state of the union, but also throughout most of the world. The plant is found along slow-moving streams and rivers and at the edges of lakes.

USES

Fresh watercress leaves have a strong spiciness—similar to a raw radish—which makes them a particularly flavorful addition to bland foods. Watercress is extremely versatile and can be used as diversely as you'd use spinach: in salads, soups, omelets, quiches, and sandwich spreads, or sautéed or steamed.

If you want to eat it raw, watercress is best collected in the spring. When the plant begins to flower in summer, its stalks, stems, and leaves become increasingly bitter and thus less suitable for raw dishes.

A bundle of watercress for sale at a farmers' market.

When collecting, do not pull up the entire plant. Instead, carefully pinch off the tender new growing tips of the plant. Rinse in cold water before you prepare your dish.

Since watercress will grow in polluted waters, if you're unsure of the water's relative purity, it would be better not to eat the greens raw. If you must eat it raw, however, then soak the greens for about 15 minutes in a dilute solution of iodine crystal water.

Primal Scream (Watercress Salad)

2 cups watercress greens, coarsely chopped
2 cups other available greens (lamb's-quarters, sow thistle, purslane, etc.)
½ cup onions or nasturtium leaves, diced
2 garlic cloves, diced

DRESSING

Salt or kelp to taste
2 tablespoons oil
2 tablespoons vinegar or lemon juice

This salad is easily made. It's an excellent complement to freshly baked fish. Blend all the ingredients and add the dressing.

MAKES FOUR MEDIUM SERVINGS.

The CCC Salad (Cumulus Cloud Carnival)

2 cups watercress leaves, coarsely chopped
1 cup loose-leaf lettuce, torn by hand into bite-size bits
1 fully ripe avocado, sliced
1 cup fennel stalks, or shepherd's purse leaves
1 cup marinated artichoke hearts or marinated asparagus tips
3 large salad tomatoes, sliced in wedges
Blue cheese dressing and fresh pepper to taste

Arrange all the ingredients in one large salad bowl or on individual plates. Chill before serving. Top with dressing, and then grind the fresh pepper over the top.

SERVES FOUR.

Wild Thomas (a Watercress Salad Dressing)

2 tablespoons lemon juice
1 teaspoon tarragon vinegar or apple cider vinegar
½ cup olive oil
1 teaspoon salt
⅛ teaspoon pepper
2 bunches of watercress leaves, finely cut

Combine all the ingredients and blend in a blender until a nearly smooth consistency is reached.

Enjoy with the memory of Wild Thomas of the Daily Bread Cafe.

SERVES TWO.

Arroyo Trout Fishing (Sautéed Watercress)

4 tablespoons butter
3 cups onions, sliced
½ cup "button" mushrooms, whole or sliced
10 cups watercress, torn into bite-size pieces
2 tablespoons (heaping) amaranth seeds
Tamari sauce to taste

Melt the butter at low temperature in a cast-iron skillet. Sauté the onions and mushrooms until slightly browned. Add the watercress and cook till the leaves are wilted.

Turn off the heat. Add the amaranth seeds and cover the skillet for 15 minutes before serving. Season with tamari sauce to taste.

This is a very simple dish that is surprisingly delicious and nutritionally wholesome (due in large part to the remarkable properties of the seeds). Serve with trout.

SERVES FOUR.

John Linthurst Special (Steamed Greens)

3 cups whole watercress
3 cups swiss chard leaves
½ red onion, sliced
Butter
Garlic powder and kelp to taste

Steam the greens and onion in a bamboo or metal steamer for 5 minutes. Serve with butter and garlic powder and kelp. This is a good balance for any "meat 'n potatoes" or other starchy dishes.

MAKES THREE MEDIUM SERVINGS.

Cress Zinger Sandwich Spread

1 cup watercress, including the stems, diced
½ cup red onion, finely diced
¼ cup young wild radish leaves, finely diced
1 teaspoon fresh (or powdered) basil
2 tablespoons homemade mayonnaise
1 cup cream cheese

Mix the ingredients well, then spread on crackers (Ak Mak, Rye Krisp, etc.) or fresh wheat bread.

MAKES ABOUT SIX SMALL SERVINGS.

Watercress greens can be cooked into a soup and added to eggs. Here, a whole meal is created with wild foods.

Mesa Verde Breakfast (Watercress Omelet)

1 cup onions or nasturtium leaves, diced
4 tablespoons butter
2 cups watercress, chopped
8 eggs
2 garlic cloves, minced
1 teaspoon paprika
1 tortilla or pita bread
Salsa

Lightly sauté the onions in butter. Add the watercress, cover, and let cook for about 2 minutes. Blend eggs, garlic, and paprika in a separate bowl and beat with a fork until frothy. Stir into watercress mixture and cook until done to your taste.

Serve on a tortilla or stuffed into a pita bread pocket. Top with a splash of salsa.

THIS WILL NOURISH SIX CHILDREN OR THREE CONSTRUCTION WORKERS.

Tongva Memories (Watercress Soup)

3 cups milk
1 cup watercress, finely minced
1 cup cream (or milk)
Paprika
1½ teaspoons salt or kelp

Heat (do not boil) 3 cups of milk, add the minced watercress, and let the mixture steep for 5 minutes covered. Add 1 cup of cream and again let simmer at low heat for 5 minutes. Ladle into bowls and sprinkle with paprika and salt or kelp. Serve with a sprig of whole watercress.

SERVES THREE.

Geauga County Express (Watercress Soup)

6 large Jerusalem artichokes (or 4 large homegrown potatoes)
3 cups water
2 cups watercress, chopped
2 garlic cloves, chopped
1 cup milk
1 tablespoon butter
1 teaspoon sea salt (or 1 tablespoon dried kelp)
1 teaspoon dill weed
1 teaspoon fresh peppercorns

Boil the Jerusalem artichokes or potatoes until tender enough to mash with a fork or potato masher. Save the water. Mash the Jerusalem artichokes or potatoes coarsely, then return to the water. Add the watercress and garlic, and cook for about 5 minutes at low heat. Turn off heat, then add the milk, butter, and seasonings. Cover the pot and let stand with the heat off for 15 minutes before serving. Serve with a slice of Amish cheese.

SERVES SIX.

WILD LETTUCE (*Lactuca serriola*)

Wild Lettuce is a member of the Sunflower family (Asteraceae). The Sunflower family has about 1,500 genera, and about 23,000 species. This is one of the largest botanical families in the world. Jepson divides this very large family into 14 groups. All plants addressed here from the Sunflower family are within "Group 8" (the Chicory Tribe), described as having ligulate heads, five-lobed ligules (five teeth per petal), and generally containing milky sap when broken.

The *Lactuca* genus contains about 100 species worldwide.

IDENTIFYING WILD LETTUCE

This plant can often grow to 6 feet tall, usually with one main stalk, but occasionally branched. The alternately arranged leaves are variable in shape. The overall shape is oblong to lanceolate, and the margin is slightly toothed. The leaf can be deeply lobed in some varieties. The leaf measures from 2 to 8 inches long. A row of spines is seen on the underside of the leaf on the midrib.

Wild lettuce, aka prickly lettuce, grows all over the United States as a common weed in gardens, fields, roadsides, backyards, and even in the cracks of urban sidewalks.

Very young prickly lettuce, at the only stage when it's suitable for salad.

A view of wild lettuce plants, showing two variations. The tall one on the left consists of more or less unlobed leaves; the one on the right has deeply lobed leaves.

Wild lettuce growing in a garden pot.

USES

Reputedly the "mother" of all cultivated lettuces, this plant can make an excellent salad if gathered young enough. If you wait too long to collect it, the plant will become bitter, spiny, and largely inedible.

Young, still-tender leaves can be collected and used as you'd use lettuce. Add tomato, vinegar and oil dressing, dill weed, and kelp. Use the young wild lettuce leaves as a main salad ingredient, or add other wild greens such as chickweed, sow thistle, miner's lettuce, or onion.

The older plants should be steamed before eating. This is to reduce any bitterness that may have developed and to soften up the spines that develop on the undersides of all the leaves. The steamed plant is good with just mild seasoning such as butter, but it can also be served with sautéed onions, hard-boiled eggs, and other cooked vegetables.

A milky sap exudes when any part of the plant is cut or broken. The stalks are generally covered with short spines.

The small flowers are yellow and similar in appearance to dandelion.

Let Us Eat Lettuce

1 cup wild lettuce leaves
1 cup lamb's-quarters leaves
1 cup mallow leaves

Steam all of the greens. Season mildly with butter and salt.

SERVES TWO.

Recipe suggested by Samuel K. Miller of Laguna Hills, California.

Spring Powerhouse

2 cups very young wild lettuce leaves (before they become bitter)
2 cups blander spring greens (lamb's-quarters, chickweed, miner's lettuce, etc.)
1 cup shepherd's purse leaves, rinsed
2 cloves garlic
½ onion (or about ½ cup wild onions, chopped)
1 carrot, sliced thin or shredded
1 tomato
1 teaspoon golden chia seeds
1 teaspoon sunflower seeds
1 teaspoon sesame seeds
Pinch of freshly ground pepper

DRESSING

Equal parts of top quality, cold-pressed oil and apple cider vinegar (use sparingly).

You probably won't be able to concoct this delicious salad when you're on the trail, but try it sometime when guests are coming over. The powerful flavor of this relatively simple salad will make you immediately aware of the limitations of the average American diet.

Blend all the ingredients, toss, and add dressing.

SERVES ABOUT FOUR.

A wild lettuce plant growing amid cactus in a dry environment.

The bottom rib of each mature leaf of wild lettuce develops the spines you see here.

Simple Cooked Lettuce Dish

1 red potato, sliced
1 green pepper, sliced
2 cups wild lettuce leaves
Approximately ⅓ cup cheddar cheese, shredded

Steam one potato and one green pepper. When almost done, add the wild lettuce leaves. When all is cooked, put into dishes and immediately sprinkle the shredded cheese over the top of the cooked vegetables.

Serve immediately.

SERVES TWO.

WILD ONION (*Allium* spp.)

Wild onions were formerly classified in the Lily family, and are now classified in the Onion and Garlic family (Alliaceae). This family contains about 13 genera and about 750 to 800 species worldwide.

The *Allium* genus contains about 700 species worldwide.

IDENTIFYING WILD ONION

Wild onions bear a strong resemblance to the green onions found in produce stores. They are grass-like plants with a leafless flower stalk. The flower has six perianth segments (indistinguishable sepals and petals).

Found all over the United States, commonly in sandy streamsides, but also in deserts, fields, and mountains, wild onions grow from 6 to 12 inches tall.

USES

Wild onions are a most versatile food since they can be added to most other foods, either raw or cooked. Onions enhance the flavor of many dishes and can be served alone as well.

A view of wild onion flowers. PHOTO BY HELEN W. NYERGES.

Onions can be added raw to salads and cooked with soups, stews, omelets, vegetable dishes, meats, and even breads.

During parts of the year, some Indian tribes relied heavily on wild onions, using them in a variety of raw and cooked dishes. Onions alone make good salad, soup, or cooked greens.

When using wild onions, remove any fibrous outer layers and then both the bulb and leaves can be eaten. The flower stalks are often too fibrous to eat.

Also included in the *Allium* genus are garlics, chives, leeks, shallots, and all domestic onions.

How can you be sure you've got an onion? Use your nose! If the plant lacks the typical onion aroma, do not

A view of the entire wild onion plant. PHOTO BY RICK ADAMS.

Wild onions often blend in with lawn grasses.

Small wild onions in the kitchen, washed, and ready to be added to a stew. Most of the little tubers were replanted. PHOTO BY HELEN W. NYERGES.

eat it unless you positively know the plant to be an edible species. There are poisonous plants that resemble onions, but they lack the aroma. Play it safe. If there's no aroma—leave it alone.

The most notable feature is the unmistakable onion-like aroma. You can safely consume any onion plant once you've crushed the leaf and detected the onion-like aroma.

Tuolumne Meadow Moonrise

2 cups onion leaves and bulbs
¼ cup water
2 cups water or milk (can be made from powdered milk)
4 cattail "bulbs," chopped into small pieces
1 large Jerusalem artichoke
2 tablespoons acorn flour (already leached of its tannic acid)
¼ cup chia seeds
Dash of salt and pepper

Cut the onions into small pieces (using only the tender portions) and put in a soup pot with ¼ cup of water. Let simmer for 5 minutes. Add the rest of the liquid and the cattail and Jerusalem artichoke.

Cook at a low temperature; do not let boil (if you are using milk). When the cattail and the Jerusalem artichoke tubers are almost done, add the acorn flour and the chia seeds. Mix them into the soup, and sprinkle in the desired amount of salt and pepper.

This recipe can be doubled if you have more guests to serve. Also, you can easily substitute potatoes for the cattails and the Jerusalem artichokes.

SERVES THREE.

Rocky Mountain Winter (Cream of Onion Soup)

2 cups wild onion bulbs and greens, cleaned and chopped fine
4 cups water
3 tablespoons whole-wheat or soy flour
2 cups milk (can be made from powdered milk)

Begin by cooking the onions in the water. In a cup, blend the flour with a little of the milk until there is a fine consistency and then pour into the soup, stirring while you pour. Add the rest of the milk and cook the soup at a low temperature for about 15 minutes.

Serve hot in mugs or in a soup bowl with toast.

SERVES FIVE.

The Sun Reflects upon the Lake

2 cups wild onion bulbs and leaves, the fibrous parts removed
2 large potatoes, diced
2 eggs
Butter
Paprika

Simmer the onions and potatoes in a covered pot with minimal water. While the potatoes and onions are cooking, hard-boil the eggs. When the vegetables and eggs are done, place the onions and potatoes in a serving dish. Peel the eggs and slice. Add the slices to the dish, and season with butter and paprika.

Serve this onion and potato dish with freshly caught and baked trout.

SERVES THREE.

Wild Cherokee Eggs

6 eggs, beaten
½ cup diced wild onion greens

Warm the skillet with olive oil. Add the eggs and cook for a few minutes. Toss in the greens and cook until done.

Season to taste; serve warm.

This is a very simple dish. When Dolores and I attended the 1989 Memorial for the Trail of Tears in Tahlequah, Oklahoma, this was served by Chief John Ketcher at the Community Feed at the end of the 3-day event. The wild onions were collected from the local fields, where they grew abundantly.

Aside from the fact that this was a delicious dish, we were very impressed by Chief Ketcher, a man who was remembered for his courage, humility, and commitment to his tribe. Chief Ketcher was right there on the outdoor food-serving line, serving up a large scoop of "Wild Cherokee Eggs" with a smile. Even though we'd only met him 2 days earlier, he treated us as if we were old friends.

SERVES TWO OR THREE.

Wake-Up Salad

1 cup wild onion leaves and bulbs
1 cup chickweed
½ cup black mustard leaves
2 tomatoes
1 lemon, juiced
1 tablespoon safflower oil
Dash of salt and pepper

Collect the onions and remove any fibrous parts. Dice and add to the salad bowl. Add the chickweed and mustard leaves, torn into bite-size pieces. Dice up two ripe tomatoes and add to the salad. Once you've squeezed in the lemon juice and poured oil and some salt and pepper into the salad bowl, toss well and serve.

Can be served with scrambled eggs.

SERVES FOUR.

WILD RADISH (*Raphanus sativus*)

Wild radish is a member of the Mustard family (Brassicaceae). The Mustard family is another large family, comprising more than 330 genera worldwide and about 3,780 species.

The *Raphanus* genus contains three species worldwide.

IDENTIFYING WILD RADISH

Wild radish is somewhat widespread in fields, gardens, and somewhat disturbed soils. The leaves are lyrately pinnately divided, like the *Brassica* leaves, though they tend to be smoother and covered with sparse stiff hairs. The flowers are lavender to white—rarely pastel yellow—and are divided in the typical Mustard family pattern: four petals, four sepals, six stamens (four tall, two short), and one pistil. The flowers are formed in racemes, and eventually pods develop. The pods somewhat resemble serrano peppers.

The root is white, generally woody, though a soft outer layer can actually be peeled and eaten.

The four-petaled flowers of the wild radish.

A view of the overall radish plant.

USES

Everything tender on the radish plant can be used for food. This means the flowers, the tender upper stems, the flower buds, the leaves (young and old), and the still-tender pods. Most parts are spicy, even spicy-hot, so when you use any parts of the plant raw in salads, you'll need to blend them with other greens or vegetables. All the tender parts of the wild radish plant are good in soups, stir-fries, cooked egg dishes, stews, and even pickled.

HEALTH NOTE

Anthony William, medical consultant, wrote an excellent blog on the benefits of radishes, which we'll summarize here.

A typical wild radish leaf.

The young, tender radish seed pods can be eaten in salads, added to cooked dishes, and pickled.

John Clarity examines the individual wild radish pods.

The entire Mustard family, of which radishes are a part, have long been known to be great cancer fighters. William points out that by including radishes in the diet, you can keep the stomach, kidneys, mouth, and colon healthy, and hopefully cancer-free.

The "spiciness" of radishes is because they are rich in vitamin C, folic acid, and anthocyanins, and this makes them great for sinus congestion, sore throats, and other ailments where an antibacterial substance is needed.

William emphasizes that it is the leaves of the radish plant that are more nutritious than the root and should be eaten.

That dovetails very well with foraging, since there isn't much of a root to harvest from the wild radish. Foragers typically only have the leaves and tender stems and flowers of radishes to use in all manner of dishes, from juices to salads, soups and stews, egg dishes, and casseroles.

Two wild radish roots, resembling carrots except that they are white and more fibrous.

Hidden Agenda

4 cups cooked brown rice
1 cup tender radish stems, diced, steamed or boiled
1 cup lamb's-quarters greens, steamed or boiled
Dr. Bronner's Liquid Amino Acids
Butter, dab

While the cooked rice is still hot and shortly before serving, blend in the radish and lamb's-quarters. Add about a teaspoon of the Dr. Bronner's Liquid Amino Acids, top with a dab of butter, and serve.

SERVES FOUR.

Rich Redman shows a one-of-a-kind wild radish root. This was grown in a wood chip pile during a very wet winter. It weighed 16 pounds.

Pickled Pods

1 cup tender young radish pods
Raw apple cider vinegar

Wash the pods and place loosely into a quart jar. Add enough raw apple cider vinegar to cover. Refrigerate for about 2 weeks before eating.

Note: You could substitute the vinegar with the juice from a can of pickled jalapeño peppers.

Daniella's Favorite Salad

1 cup tender wild radish flowers, tender upper stems, and leaves
1 cup young chickweed
1 cup lamb's-quarters leaves
Vinaigrette dressing

Rinse the greens and chop or tear them into bite-size pieces. Add dressing and serve.

Optional: Add diced tomatoes or sliced avocado pieces.

SERVES FOUR.

Nuts (and Seeds)

AMARANTH (*Amaranthus* spp.)

Amaranth is a member of the Amaranth family (Amaranthaceae), which has about 75 genera and 900 species worldwide.

Oscar Duardo stands in front of a patch of cultivated erect amaranths. These are primarily used for the seed, though the leaves can be cooked and eaten too.

An amaranth
whose seeds
are nearly
mature.

A bowl of the white amaranth seed from the cultivated varieties of the plant.

Black amaranth seed from one of the wild varieties of the plant.

There are about 70 species of genus *Amaranthus* worldwide. Pigweed or red-root (*Amaranthus retroflexus*) is perhaps the most commonly used species here in the United States.

Read about how to identify amaranth in the Greens section, page 22.

Amaranth is a tasty and versatile seed, used in soups, chips, pastry products, breads, and pancakes. You can begin using the seeds by simply adding a small amount to various dishes.

Here is one recipe that I like.

Amaranth Halvah

1 cup amaranth seed
Honey

Grind 1 cup of amaranth seed to a fine powder. This can be done with a primitive stone grinder or a modern kitchen blender. Mix with honey until you reach a halvah-like consistency. You can form this into balls and roll the balls in the whole amaranth seeds.

This is a very tasty trail snack. Works best with the white amaranth seeds.

SERVES UP TO TWENTY, DEPENDING ON THE SIZE OF THE BALLS MADE.

LAMB'S-QUARTERS (*Chenopodium album*)

Lamb's-quarters is a member of the Goosefoot family (Chenopodiaceae), which includes 100 genera and 1,500 species worldwide. The *Chenopodium* genus contains about 100 species worldwide.

Read about how to identify lamb's-quarters in the Greens section, page 22.

USES

Lamb's-quarters seed is harvested when the annual plant is dying, or fully dead. When you pull off a handful of the seed heads and rub them between your hands, you can blow off the chaff. If you are left with a handful of the black seeds, you know you can go ahead and harvest the seeds.

We harvest all we can when it's in season, and then manually remove all the stems and debris. We fill a large salad bowl about halfway with the seeds. Then we rub the seeds by hand to remove the dry outer chaff. By gently shaking the salad bowl, and gently blowing onto the seeds, you can blow off the chaff, little by little. You want to end up with mostly the pure black seed.

In general, seeds are mixed with other seeds to make pastry and bread products, and are added to soups.

All the leaves have died back on this *Chenopodium album*, leaving only the seeds, which can now be easily harvested.

Earth Bread

1 cup lamb's-quarters seeds
1 cup acorn flour
3 teaspoons baking powder
1 teaspoon sea salt
3 tablespoons honey
1 egg
1 cup raw milk
3 tablespoons oil

The lamb's-quarters seeds can be gathered in abundance in late summer and fall when the leaves have withered away and the seed clusters are brown. Once collected, winnow away any remaining chaff and foreign matter. I've used the seeds immediately upon harvesting, but there are other options. You can roast and grind the seeds, or you can soak the seeds in water for about an hour before using.

Mix all the ingredients together and bake in an oiled pan for about 30 minutes (or until done) in an oven set at 300°F. If you're cooking over a fire, put the batter into a pan and then invert a larger pan over the first. Bake over the coals of your fire.

Another possibility with this recipe is to thin it with water or milk to the consistency of pancake batter and then make pancakes. Serve the pancakes with honey or wild jelly.

I've served this Earth Bread to many foragers and have had mixed responses. A few people did not like it, and said it tasted "like dirt," an honest response that I regarded as refreshing.

Some were surprised at its unique flavor. There have also been ecstatic responses from people who found the bread to be "virile," "basic," "deliciously wholesome and sustaining," "primitive," and "amazing." These smiling and laughing bread samplers were often at a loss to describe this dark, nutty, heavy bread.

Suggestion: Add raisins and chopped walnuts to the batter. Carry the bread along during your travels, whether to the deep wilderness or to the factory. Cut thin slices from the loaf and chew slowly and completely. We believe you will find this Earth Bread sustaining and satisfying. Whole-wheat flour can substitute for the acorn flour.

MAKES ABOUT TWELVE SLICES.

A bowl of harvested and winnowed lamb's-quarters seed.

Wild Backyard Soup

Your normal pot of vegetable soup
½ cup lamb's-quarters seeds, cleaned

When your regular pot of soup is nearly done, add ½ cup of lamb's-quarters seeds. They will swell up a little so you'll know they are done (but they do not swell up as much as the related quinoa seed).

There is a distinct flavor that the lamb's-quarters seed adds, and so you should add more or less seeds depending on your preferences.

WALNUTS

The black walnut (*Juglans* spp.) and English walnut (*Juglans regia*) are members of the Walnut family (Juglandaceae). The Walnut family contains nine genera and about 60 species worldwide.

IDENTIFYING WALNUTS

The black walnut is widespread in North America, in canyons, valleys, and hillsides.

Additionally, you may encounter the English walnut either planted in yards or surviving around old farms and cabins.

This is a full-bodied native deciduous tree with pinnately divided leaves. There are typically from 11 to 19 leaflets per leaf.

Keith Farrar next to a black walnut tree with immature green nuts.

Green (immature) walnuts in the tree.

The mature black walnuts in the tree.

As the nuts begin their development, they are covered with a green outer layer. This layer matures into a mushy texture and turns black. This black outer layer is also a very good dye, so you should wear gloves if you are collecting the nuts while the outer layer is still "wet," or just collect after the walnuts have dried.

You will need to crack open the nuts with a rock or a hammer. If you crack it from the top, you're more likely to get an even split, which will make it easier to extract the meat.

The meat in the black walnut is oily and delicious, though there's not as much meat as you'd find in the cultivated English walnut.

USES

The meat of walnuts was widely used by all the Native American tribes who had access to it. Sometimes it was mixed with other seeds and berries to make a type of bread. The nutmeats were added to various soups, such as

A view of collected black walnuts and cracked walnuts in the molcajete. Note the amount of nutmeat compared to shell.

corn soup. Sometimes, the nutmeats were crushed, boiled, and the oil allowed to come to the top. The walnut oil was then used for various recipes.

You can also use a little nut pick to separate out the shell from the meat. This could take a while to get enough walnuts for a cake, cookie, or other dessert items.

FORAGER NOTES

The green, immature black walnuts were once crushed and tossed into pools of water by the indigenous peoples to stun the fish. Then the fish would be scooped out by hand or with nets.

ACORNS (*Quercu* spp. and *Notholithocarpus densiflorus*)

Acorns are a member of the Oak family (Fagaceae). Worldwide, the *Quercus* genus (oak trees) includes about 500 species. Oak trees are common and widespread in North America. At least 90 species are found in the United States, and when you include species from Canada and Mexico, the number is well over a hundred different species.

IDENTIFYING ACORNS

Acorns are the nuts of the oak tree. Each acorn has a scaly cap. Depending on the species of oak tree, each acorn is a bit different, and yet every child can recognize an acorn! The oak trees are deciduous or evergreen, with some being bushes, though most are very large trees.

Acorns in the tree.

Mature acorns ready to be processed.

David Martinez grinds raw acorns into a flour.

David Martinez pours water through the ground acorns to remove the bitter tannic acid.

Raw acorn flour has been placed into a sieve that is lined with a tea cloth. Cold water is poured through the acorn flour until it is no longer bitter.

Oak trees are found in most environments. Most are large trees, but some are bush-like, such as the scrub oak. Some are evergreen (the "live" oaks), and some are deciduous, such as the black oak, red oak, and valley oak. Oaks are inherently beautiful. They were a source of food and survival to the indigenous peoples who lived here for millennia, using the natural foods of the land.

In the fall of most years, acorns drop from the trees, often in great numbers. Some years are better than others.

In the past, acorns would be collected, dried, and stored, and then processed as needed.

Acorns generally fall from the trees beginning in late September, and can still fall into January. It is best to collect the acorns off the ground so you know they are mature.

USES

If you don't have the time to process acorns right after gathering, you should at least dry them so they do not get moldy and so that larvae does not develop. Lay them on cookie sheets in the full sun for a few days, or place them in an oven where a pilot light will help to dry them.

When you're ready to begin cooking with acorns, your first step is to shell them. If your acorns are dry, you can place each acorn on a flat rock and hit it with a rock, and the shell will come off easily. You can try whatever works for you—a rock, a hammer, a piece of wood.

Then the acorns must be processed to remove the tannic acid, and there are several ways you can do this.

At an acorn processing workshop, acorns are shelled, ground on a metate, and leached (foreground).

Let's look at the expedient way to process acorns first. Shell the acorns and put them into your pot. Cover with water and bring to a boil. Within a few minutes, the water will look like mud as the tannic acid comes out of the acorns. Dump the water and add fresh water. Bring to a boil again. Rinse, and do it again. How long do you do this? Since each variety of acorn has a different

The author cooks up a batch of acorn pancakes. PHOTO BY HELEN NYERGES.

amount of tannic acid, you must periodically taste one of the acorns. Still bitter? OK, do another boiling. When you taste the acorn and it's just bland with no bitterness, it should be done.

When the acorns are leached, you could actually just toss them in a pot with vegetables and seasonings, and make a stew. Or, if you're out camping, you might mash up the leached acorns on a rock, and use it as a thickener for a soup or stew.

Acorn pancakes from a workshop, ready to be enjoyed with some jelly.

If you're at home and you try this method, you could also run the acorns through a meat grinder to reduce them to a coarse meal, and then process them into a finer meal, as needed.

You could also try processing the acorns in a method that is more akin to the way it was done by the indigenous peoples of native California, the method that I prefer today.

First, the acorns are shelled, and then I grind them on a flat metate, as they were done in the old days. Next, I line a colander with a piece of cotton (I prefer a tea cloth), and put in the ground acorn meal. I pour hot water through the acorn meal and let it filter through the cotton, taking the tannic acid out with it. It is likely to take several pourings to get out all the bitterness.

The time required to leach the acorns is partly a factor of how bitter the acorns are in the first place, which is determined by species. It's also a factor of what sort of cotton you use for the filter. Don't use a tight-weave cotton fabric, like a pillowcase, since it will take too long for the water to filter through. You should use something like a cotton kerchief or the tea cloth.

PROCESSING/COOKING

I make pancakes, biscuits, or cookies with acorns. For pancakes or biscuits, I use half acorn flour to half whole-wheat or mixed-grain flour. I add more water to the pancake batter, and less to the biscuit mix. For cookies, I use the same blend, often adding raisins or peanut butter.

Barbara's Acorn Pound Cake

½ cup olive oil
¾ cup sugar or ½ cup honey
2 eggs
½ cup acorn flour
1¼ cups whole-wheat flour
⅛ teaspoon salt
½ teaspoon cream of tartar
¼ teaspoon baking soda
¼ cup milk
½ teaspoon vanilla extract
¼ teaspoon mace or ½ teaspoon nutmeg

Mix together the olive oil, sugar or honey, eggs, and acorn flour. In a second mixture, combine the flour, salt, cream of tartar, and baking soda. Stir the second mixture into the first, a little at a time, alternating with the milk, vanilla extract, and mace/nutmeg.

Beat it all well. Pour batter into a prepared 8-inch square or round pan or a bread pan. Bake at 350°F for 50 to 60 minutes.

REFERENCES

WILD FOOD BOOKS BY CHRISTOPHER NYERGES

Books by FalconGuides:
Foraging California
Nuts and Berries of California
Foraging Oregon
Foraging Washington
Foraging Idaho
Foraging Arizona
Foraging Virginia, Maryland, and Washington DC
Guide to Wild Foods and Useful Plants, Chicago Review Press.
Extreme Simplicity: Homesteading in the City, Dover Press. Includes sections on urban foraging.
Self-Sufficient Home, Stackpole Books. Includes sections on foraging.
Enter the Forest, School of Self-Reliance. Includes sections on native uses of plants.
How to Survive Anywhere, Stackpole Books. Includes a chapter on wild foods.

OTHER FALCON FORAGING GUIDES
Foraging New York, by Steven Brill

OTHER SUGGESTED REFERENCES
The Edible Wild: A Complete Cookbook and Guide to Edible Wild Plants in Canada and North America, by Berudt Berglund and Clare E. Bolsby. Charles Scribner's Sons, 1971.
The Scout's Guide to Wild Edibles, by Mike Krebil. St. Lynn's Press, 2016.
Beachcomber's Handbook, by Euell Gibbons. David McKay, 1967.
Native American Ethnobotany, by Daniel E. Moerman. Timber Press, 1998.
Botany in a Day, by Thomas Elpel. HOPS Press, 1996.
Healing with Medicinal Plants of the West, by James Adams, Enrique Villaseñor, and Michelle Wong. Abedus Press, 2012.

REMEMBERING EUELL GIBBONS
(1911–1975)

In the late 1960s and early 1970s, a wave of ecological and "back to the land" awareness swept the country. This period saw the rise of the incredibly popular *Mother Earth News* magazine, communes, and Euell Gibbons.

Euell Gibbons was a man of modest means who loved to fish and forage, and who always wanted to be a writer. His first work was a novel about a man who tried to live off the land by eating common weeds that grow everywhere. But Gibbons's publisher told him to rewrite the book from a novel to a guidebook for identifying these wayside plants. That book was *Stalking the Wild Asparagus*, first published in 1962, and by the early 1970s, it had become a bestseller, along with several other books by the aging naturalist.

By 1974, Gibbons began to capitalize on his popularity and became the frontman for Post Grape-Nuts, a cereal that contained no grapes and no nuts. The Post company flew Gibbons around the country to make commercials in diverse areas. Gibbons would first be brandishing a pine cone, or cattails, or goldenrod flowers, and then he'd often have cereal with a group at their outdoor

Christopher Nyerges (right) meets Euell Gibbons at a press conference at Pasadena City College in 1975.

breakfast table. Of course, they'd be eating only Grape-Nuts, with Gibbons's final and famous line being, "Reminds me of wild hickory nuts."

Gibbons had somehow tapped into an ancient knowledge that America was ready for, and hungry for—the knowledge of how to use the acres and acres of wild-growing plants that were both edible and medicinal. Not only did Gibbons share the ancient knowledge of Native Americans, but also the knowledge of wild plants from most of the world, since the common weeds currently growing in North America originally came from Europe, as well as many from Asia and Africa.

Gibbons was born in Texas on September 8, 1911, and spent his childhood in northwestern New Mexico. He describes how his family moved from place to place with his father's job, and how their income was sporadic. At an early age, Gibbons began to collect wild greens and fruits to supplement the family's meals. He was only 15 when he left home and took jobs as a cowboy and carpenter. He was living in California during the Dust Bowl, and he describes himself as a hobo during that era.

Background

He served in the US Army and later worked as a carpenter and boat-builder. He was married and divorced, describing his first marriage as a "casualty of the war." By World War II, Gibbons was living in Hawaii, and worked building and repairing boats for the US Navy. At age 36, he entered the University of Hawaii as an anthropology student. It was there that he got more serious about writing, and where he met his second wife, Freda, whom he married in 1948.

By 1953, Gibbons and Freda had moved to Pennsylvania where he lived and pursued his writing aspirations. His first book was published in 1962. Once he began doing commercials for Post Grape-Nuts in the early 1970s, the popularity of his books skyrocketed, and Gibbons became a household name.

Eventually, Gibbons was regularly seen on nearly every talk show in the country, especially Johnny Carson's *Tonight Show*. Even when Gibbons wasn't on the show, Carson joked about Gibbons's use of wild foods so often that Gibbons became a household name.

Gibbons wrote articles for *National Geographic*, regular columns for various newspapers and magazines such as *Organic Gardening* magazine, and lectured far and wide. Each of his books was very popular, and included new information about another aspect of foraging.

The many books by Gibbons were popular partly because of his personality, and partly because there were scant few books about how to identify and use wild plants at that time. And the side effect of being so wildly popular was that he was the constant butt of all the comedians' jokes. (Gibbons laughed all the way to the bank.)

Federal Trade Commission Nixes Gibbons's Commercials

By the summer of 1975, the Federal Trade Commission had ordered Gibbons's commercials for Post Grape-Nuts cereal off the air. Gibbons died later that year, on December 29, 1975, the result of a ruptured aortic aneurysm, which was a complication of Marfan syndrome.

Gibbons had a valuable message for America: There are tons of wild, nutritious foods growing everywhere in this country that we could—but don't—eat. Gibbons believed that the main reason that Americans shun wild food is fear of ridicule if they stoop to gather weeds, which are generally regarded as suitable only for the trashcan, not the dinner table.

The FTC ruling appeared to speak to a deeper fear: fear of the unknown. In the cereal commercials, Gibbons spoke of his years of foraging for wild food. "Ever eat a pine tree?" he asked in one spot. "Many parts are edible. Natural ingredients are important to me. That's why Post Grape-Nuts is part of my breakfast."

The FTC objected to the apparent connection, especially as it might be interpreted by children. The ruling said that the commercials "undercut a commonly recognized safety principle—namely, that children should not eat any plants found growing in natural surroundings, except under adult supervision."

Yet Gibbons always stressed in his books and countless public appearances that you should never eat any plant or part of a plant until you recognize it as edible.

Gibbons's death at the age of 64 seemed to seal his reputation as a "kook." At worst, people suspected that he had accidentally poisoned himself (he hadn't); at best, it appeared that eating "natural" foods did not contribute to longevity. But those of us who saw the real value of Gibbons's teachings still feel that he left us with a precious legacy.

How Gibbons Influenced Me

I first encountered Gibbons in 1972, through his writings. I was working in a local library at the time, and I would constantly check out Gibbons's books and try to identify local plants. Excited and fascinated by *Stalking the Wild Asparagus* and his other books, I explored fields and woods across the country in search of wild edibles. I used other books as well, took classes in botany in high school, and attended lectures on ethnobotany whenever possible.

By 1974, a local nonprofit asked me to lead a Wild Food Outing to teach the subject, and I have continued to lead walks to teach about wild plants ever since.

When Gibbons came to town to give a lecture at Pasadena City College, as the press asked him questions afterward I was asked to sit with him as "Pasadena's Euell Gibbons." Gibbons was a friendly, curious, and open man. We chatted for the better part of an hour, our conversation ranging from carob pods to

American Indians to compost. He told me of his plans for television documentaries about primitive societies that still live totally ecological lives. Gibbons said he hoped to show the modern world some of the follies of civilization.

One of these follies, he told me, is the persistence—the expenditure of so much time and money—in attempting to eradicate from our yards and parks plants that have thrived for centuries. Some of the most common edible "intruders" are dandelion, lamb's-quarters, pigweed, mallow, mustard, and sow thistle. Among the most enduring of wild plants that were brought to California in the westward migrations is chickweed. To even the most pampered palate, it is an incredibly good salad green, yet it often leads the list of "garden pests" in advertisements for herbicides. Other "enemies" highly valued by herbalists and naturalists are wild garlic, plantain, sour grass, and purslane.

Gibbons was passing along something that our ancestors knew, something that is still a deeply respected tradition in many parts of even the "civilized" world, where scarce food is more prized than ornamental gardens. Despite the ridicule of passersby, on almost any day in almost any park right here in the city, people still gather berries, cactus, mustard greens, chickweed, and wild mushrooms.

Euell Gibbons and his many adherents warrant our admiration, not our mockery. Nearly every "wild food educator" today has some direct or indirect lineage to Euell Gibbons.

Books by Euell Gibbons
Stalking the Wild Asparagus (1962)
Stalking the Blue-Eyed Scallop (1964)
Stalking the Wild Herbs (1966)
Stalking the Good Life (1966)
Beachcomber's Handbook (1967)
A Wild Way to Eat (1967) [booklet for Hurricane Island Outward Bound School]
Stalking the Faraway Places (1973)
Feast on a Diabetic Diet (1973)
Euell Gibbons Handbook of Edible Wild Plants (1979) [coauthor finished after Gibbons died]

So What Sort of Person Was Gibbons?
A survivalist? No, though he loved to camp and fish.
A nutritionist? No, he used plenty of white sugar, and loved to deep fry.
A health food enthusiast? No, just read his own recipes.
A prepper? Nope.

A communist? Nope. During the Depression, he was fond of communist litera-
ture, but denounced communism by World War II.

A Quaker? Yes. After marrying Freda, he joined the Society of Friends. As Gibbons put it, "I became a Quaker because it was the only group I could join
without pretending to beliefs that I didn't have or concealing beliefs that I
did have."

A vegetarian? Nope. Read his books. He ate all manner of wildlife from the
land, sea, and air.

A pragmatic wild food enthusiast? Yes. At the core, Gibbons loved to live off
the land, making delicious meals from what nature provided.

Nutritional Composition of Wild Foods

The data below are per 100 grams, unless otherwise indicated. Blanks denote no data available; dashes denote lack of data for a constituent believed to be present in measurable amounts. Only a select number of plants for which we had data are represented.

Plant	Calories	Protein (g)	Fat (g)	Calcium (mg)	Phosphorus (mg)	Iron (mg)	Sodium (mg)	Potassium (mg)	Vitamin A (IU)	Thiamine (mg)	Riboflavin (mg)	Niacin (mg)	Vit. C (mg)	Part
Amaranth	36	3.5	0.5	267	67	3.9	—	411	6,100	0.08	0.16	1.4	80	Leaf, raw
Carob		4.5		352	81	2.9	35	827	14		0.4	1.89	0.2	Pods
Cattail		8%	2%											Rhizomes
Chia		20.2%		631	860	7.72	16	407	54	0.62	0.17	8.8	1.6	Seed
CHICORY TRIBE														
Chicory	20	1.8	0.3	86	40	0.9	—	420	4,000	0.06	0.1	0.5	22	Leaf, raw
Dandelion	45	2.7	0.7	187	66	3.1	76	397	14,000	0.19	0.26	—	35	Leaf, raw
Sow thistle	20	2.4	0.3	93	35	3.1	—	—	2,185	0.7	0.12	0.4	5	Leaf, raw
Chickweed	29.09	1.43	2.4	84	—	4.97	—	—	2,282	0.02	0.14	0.51	31	Leaf, raw
Dock	28	2.1	0.3	66	41	1.6	5	338	12,900	0.09	0.22	0.5	119	Leaf, raw
Fennel	28	2.8	0.4	100	51	2.7	—	397	3,500	—	—	—	31	Leaf, raw
Filaree	—	2.5	—	—	—	—	—	—	7,000	—	—	—	—	Leaf
Grass										300 to 500 IU	2,000 to 2,800 IU		300 to 700 mg	Leaf, raw
Lamb's quarter	43	4.2	0.8	309	72	1.2	43	452	11,600	0.16	0.44	1.2	80	Leaf, raw
Mallow	37	4.4	0.6	249	69	12.7	—	—	2,190	0.13	0.2	1.0	35	Leaf
Milkweed	—	0.8	0.5	—	—	—	—	—	—	—	—	—	—	Leaf
Miner's lettuce						10% RDA			22% RDA				33% RDA	Leaf
MUSTARD FAMILY														
Mustard	31	3	0.5	183	50	3	32	377	7,000	0.12	0.22	0.8	97	Leaf
Shepherd's purse	33	4.2	0.5	208	86	4.8	—	394	1,554	0.08	0.17	0.4	36	Leaf
Watercress	19	2.2	0.3	120	60	0.2	41	330	3,191		0.12	0.2	43	Leaf

Nasturtium														
Nettle	65	5.5	0.7	481	71	1.64	4	334	2,011	—	0.16	0.38	76	Leaf
New Zealand spinach	19	2.2	0.3	58	46	2.6	159	795	4,300	0.04	0.17	0.6	30	Leaf, raw
Oak (acorn flour)	65% carbohydrates	6%	18%	43	103	1.21	0	712	51	0.1	0.1	2.3	0	Nut
ONION FAMILY														
Chives	28	1.8	0.3	69	44	1.7	—	250	5,800	0.08	0.13	0.5	56	Leaf, raw
Garlic	137	6.2	0.2	29	202	1.5	19	529	—	0.25	0.08	0.5	15	Clove, raw
Onion	36	1.5	0.2	51	39	1	5	231	2,000	0.05	0.05	0.4	32	Young leaf, raw
Passion fruit (per pound)				31	151	3.8	66	831	1,650				71	Fruit
Pinyon	635	12	60.5		604	5.2				1.28				Nut
Prickly pear	42	0.5	0.1	20	28	0.3	2	166	60	0.01	0.03	0.4	22	Fruit, raw
Purslane	21	30	1.7	0.4	103	39	3.5	—	—	2,500	0.03	0.1	0.5	Leaf & stem, raw
Rose	162	1.6		169	61	1.06	4	429	4,345		0.16	1.3	426	Fruit, raw
SEAWEED														
Dulse	—	—	3.2	296	267	—	2,085	8,060	—	—	—	—	—	Leaf
Irish moss	—	—	1.8	885	157	8.9	2,892	2,844	—	—	—	—	—	Leaf
Kelp	—	—	1.1	1,093	240	—	3,007	5,273	—	—	—	—	—	Leaf

Primary source: *Composition of Foods*, US Department of Agriculture.

INDEX

RECIPE INDEX

ABOUT THE AUTHOR

Christopher Nyerges, cofounder of the School of Self-Reliance, has led wild-food walks for thousands of students since 1974. He has authored nearly two dozen books on wild foods, survival, and self-reliance, and thousands of newspaper and magazine articles. He continues to teach where he lives in Los Angeles County, California. His website is www.SchoolofSelf-Reliance.com.